THIS HOLY CALLING

DAILY WISDOM
FROM
WOMEN IN MINISTRY

WESLEYAN HOLINESS WOMEN CLERGY

wesleyan
PUBLISHING HOUSE
wphstore.com
Fishers, IN

Copyright © 2022 by Wesleyan Publishing House and Education & Clergy Development of
The Wesleyan Church
Published by Wesleyan Publishing House
13300 Olio Road, Suite 100
Fishers, Indiana 46037 USA.

Compiled by Priscilla Hammond, PhD, for Wesleyan Holiness Women Clergy.

Printed in the United States of America.

ISBN: 978-1-63257-463-3
ISBN (e-book): 978-1-63257-464-0

CONTENTS

FOREWORD

I had the unique privilege to read through most of these daily reflections on our shared holy calling and, frankly, my eyes were moist as I read. The thought kept going over and over in my mind: "I think this is a devotional the women who were at Pentecost and those they impacted throughout the Roman Empire would have written." I celebrate the diversity of voices represented in these pages—voices of varying marital and parenting experiences, stages of life, and ethnic, geographic, and economic experience. They enliven my imagination of God's Church as the Spirit intended at Pentecost.

I kept hearing the voice of Junia as she was planting the church in Rome, where the Roman philosophers taught that if anyone showed any type of mercy, they had a character flaw. Yet, she was undaunted. The theme of mercy runs through these writings at a time in our current culture when mercy and justice are losing more and more of their value. I was reminded of Lydia in some of the writings, as personal experiences of risk and losing all to follow our Lord were expressed. Then here came Priscilla as I listened to excellent exposition of the word of God, especially in understanding the work of the Holy Spirit in our lives. Themes of justice run boldly through these pages, and I thought of Perpetua, a young woman and mother in North Africa who defied the systems of injustice in AD 203—an early Christian martyr. Holy calling, indeed. Then, the reflections on leadership reminded me of Phoebe, a leader in the early church as noted by Paul himself.

But then my mind traveled to the Wesleyan holiness heritage and tradition which all the writers in this compilation share. I was in the company of Susanna Wesley, who courageously started a Sunday evening service in her house, preaching to crowded listeners, regularly up to two hundred people in attendance. I found myself hearing her "amen!" to each reflection. As we remember, her Anglican clergy husband did not promote women preaching, but when he saw her success, he capitulated.

Throughout these pages, I hear the fruit of B. T. Roberts' book *Ordaining Women*, in which the founder of the Free Methodist Church wrote about the equality of women extending into church, society, and the home. Then the rambunctious words of Seth C. Rees (founder of The Wesleyan Church antecedent The Pilgrim Holiness Church) make one smile or cringe depending on one's bent: "Nothing but jealousy, prejudice and bigotry and a stingy love for bossing in men have prevented women's public recognition by the church. No church that is acquainted with the Holy Ghost will object to the public ministry of women."[1]

I remember the women of the Church of the Nazarene who pastored the entire West Tennessee Conference in the early 1900s. Yes, they received some criticism, but in 1905 they responded with a book of defense entitled *Women Preachers*, as Timothy Smith described in his 1962 book, *Called unto Holiness*. Both The Wesleyan Church and the Church of God (Anderson) [USA] ordained women by the late 1800s. The first woman ordained in the United States was ordained in 1853 by the founder of the Wesleyan Methodist Church, Luther Lee; the woman— Antoinette Brown. By 1894, evangelist Julia Foote was the first woman ordained a deacon in the historic Black AME Zion denomination and in 1899 became the second woman ordained an elder in it.

From its inception in the late 1800s, the Church of God ordained both women and minorities. During the days of the Reconstruction Era of the United States, the Church of God moved women into prominent positions of church leadership.

To my knowledge, *This Holy Calling* is the first of its kind as a compilation of reflections by clergywomen from the Wesleyan holiness tradition. It is rich, Spirit-anointed, and poised for the twenty-first century. I keep thinking of the words of Phoebe Palmer in her book *The Promise of the Father*. I believe these writings and the vast public ministry represented by the women in this book are an answer to her prayer in 1859; I am humbled to be counted in their numbers:

"The church in many places is a sort of potter's field, where the gifts of woman, as so many strangers, are buried. How long, O Lord, how long before man shall roll away the stone that we may see a resurrection?"[2]

Dr. Jo Anne Lyon
General Superintendent Emerita
The Wesleyan Church

---

1. Seth C. Rees, *The Ideal Pentecostal Church* (1897), 41.
2. Phoebe Palmer, *The Promise of the Father* (1859), 347.

CALLED AS IMAGE BEARERS

THE REVELATION RADIATED IN GOOD WORKS

"We are not stoning you for any good work," they replied,
"but for blasphemy, because you, a mere man, claim to be God." (John 10:33)

The idea that Jesus and the Father are one was not something easily accepted by the religious leaders of Jesus' day. As a matter of fact, the statement revolted them, so they rejected Jesus. While Jesus' ministry frustrated the religious leaders, they were still seeing God at work. But even confronted with Jesus' good works, they couldn't bring themselves to believe that Jesus might really be the Son of God.

You don't have to be a Christian to do good things; there are plenty of people who like to do good. You also don't have to "do good works" to be reconciled to God. But when you are united with Christ, you are driven to do good works because of the nature of Christ at work in you. What is revealed in your own behavior is Christ in you.

When we are in Christ, we may also experience a similar response from those around us, to our actions, behaviors, and words. Without claiming to be God, we may face hostility just by claiming to be called by God. This certainly happens for women clergy; there are those who declare our ministry blasphemous. But we will not be deterred, continuing in communion with our triune God who delights in our faithfulness. And as a result of this, we can't help but be engaged in doing good, even in the face of opposition. Our good works aren't meant to promote ourselves but to radiate the glory of Christ through the joy of the Spirit. In this way, our preaching and faithful living will reveal God to the world.

—CARLA SUNBERG

TODAY

Spend time with our triune God so Christ is revealed in your activities.

THE VISIBLE IMAGE OF LOVE

The Son is the image of the invisible God, the firstborn
over all creation. (Col. 1:15)

There is so much about God that is difficult for us to understand or explain. Jesus "is the image of the invisible God." In the Son, we see the invisible nature of God made visible. It's not the physical image of the Trinity that we see, but rather the very perfect image of the heart of the Trinity, which is revealed in Christ.

If we are going to reflect the image, then we need to absorb a little more about the image. It is this perfect image we are called to carry into the world—the nature of the invisible God! Picture a mirror: the closer a mirror is to a person, the larger the person will be in that mirror. The closer we draw to Christ, the more we will reflect Christ's nature. Do you see too little of God's nature at work in the world these days? It's not that God is absent; but it may be that we are too distant from God.

To get to know God, we need to soak in the scriptures, spend time in prayer, and worship with God's people. This isn't just time preparing for sermons or teaching. As you personally seek the face of God for yourself, you will be continually drawn nearer to the image. When you draw close to Christ, you become like a musical instrument that God plays to share the song of the Trinity.

—CARLA SUNBERG

TODAY

Look for ways you can make the image of God's love visible.

9

WELCOME TO THE NEW ERA OF INCARNATE LOVE

On that day you will realize that I am in my Father,
and you are in me, and I am in you. (John 14:20)

The 1965 song "What the World Needs Now Is Love" was hugely popular when it was released. While the secular song was a hit, the premise remains true for our world today—what we need is love! And when Jesus was born, he ushered in a new era, revealing God's heart of holy love.

I'll always remember the first year my husband and I celebrated Christmas without our grown daughters. It had long been our practice to invite others into our home on Christmas, welcoming them like they were part of our family. But that year, we had been in our new ministry for a month, living in temporary housing, when Christmas arrived. It was then that our usual practice of hospitality was turned upside down: we were invited into someone else's home. It was a new era, but we felt loved and welcomed to a new part of the country.

Jesus took on flesh so we would have the privilege of being loved into a new family. Today we can be called children of God! We welcome Emmanuel, God with us, but also God in us. The world needs "love, sweet love," as the song goes, and Christ followers should be oozing with God's love. The gift we receive in Christ overflows to our world through you and me. Why? Because Jesus is in the Father, the Father is in him, and, through the Holy Spirit, Christ is in us—and all of this because of love.

—CARLA SUNBERG

TODAY

Welcome a new era of love from God's heart flowing through you.

RESEMBLING THE IMAGE OF GOD

Produce fruit in keeping with repentance. . . . Now Jesus . . .
was the son, so it was thought, of Joseph. (Luke 3:8, 23)

The words "produce fruit" instantly grab our attention. It doesn't matter who your parents are or if you ever knew them, it's you who are called to "produce fruit" in your own life. No one can "ride the coattails" of their parents. Similarly, no one bears responsibility for their parents' bad choices, either. It is your life alone that you answer for; your life is called to "produce fruit."

John the Baptist told religious leaders their connection to Abraham would not be what identified them as God's children. Instead, to be identified as God's child, your life had to produce fruit, "fruit worthy of repentance." This was a novel idea to his audience. Surely they were God's children; their genealogy could prove it! But John preached that bearing the family resemblance occurred by producing fruit. God would change the paradigm so that even those with no heritage from Abraham could produce fruit as God's children.

What does this fruit look like? Spirit-filled children, producing the fruit of the Spirit. That is why God's children begin to look like and act like God.

I am proud of my own father and love him dearly. He's a good man who loved and nurtured me and provided an excellent example. However, as much as I love my father, I know that ultimately I am called to resemble our heavenly Creator.

From the fruit in your life, whom do you resemble?

—CARLA SUNBERG

TODAY

Remove fruit in your life that doesn't resemble God's image.

THE IMAGE OF FORGIVENESS

"This is how my heavenly Father will treat each of you unless you forgive
your brother or sister from your heart." (Matt. 18:35)

Forgiveness is found in God's character of love, so we can expect to find it reflected in God's children. The Creator's love for humanity was revealed in his extravagant plan for forgiveness and redemption. Note that Jesus refers to "my" Father—not "our" Father. If I refuse to participate in the family mission, I lose out on relationship with my heavenly Father and Christ my brother.

It's so easy to slip into a critical spirit. The twenty-four-hour news cycle provides a simple path to negativity. Whether through a screen or fretting over how we've been wronged, little by little, our thoughts are consumed by an attitude that corrodes our relationship with God and others. Instead of basking in the love of God who delights in his children, we slip toward the downward spiral of criticism. Suddenly, there is nothing good in our thoughts left to be said. The conversation changes: "our" heavenly Father becomes an unfamiliar stranger. If you and I allow our attitudes to be overwhelmed by others' harmful attitudes and actions, ultimately, we destroy our relationship with God. In the long run, we are the ones who suffer.

God lavishes radiant love and forgiveness on us. Of all the times we fall short, God loves us anyhow. When you and I weren't looking for restored relationship, the Word became flesh so we could find our way home to the heart of the Trinity. If God did all this for me and you, then, through the power of the Holy Spirit, what will we choose to do for others?

—CARLA SUNBERG

TODAY

Pray for the loving grace of God to empower you for forgiveness.

PERFECTLY RELATED

Be perfect, therefore, as your heavenly Father is perfect. (Matt. 5:48)

There is always a relational aspect to sin and its inward curve toward self: it damages relationships. Our relationship with God is damaged. But when our relationship with God is in alignment, we are set free to be face-to-face with God. We become a reflection of God to the world. When we live face-to-face with God, God challenges us to be "perfect." This isn't about human perfection or absolute flawlessness. Rather, the root of this Greek word in Matthew is *telos*. The *telos* of something is its goal or completion, end or aim. Our goal is to become what God created us to be: a perfect or complete reflection of Triune love. This comes through repentance, turning away from our inward-curving sin, and moving toward the goal of our lives, which is Christ.

Through sin, our relationships with others are also damaged. When Adam and Eve sinned, their relationship with God changed; so did their relationship with each other. They were no longer equal partners, but Eve was now subservient to Adam. This was not God's *telos* for humanity, but rather the fallout of sin-corrupted relationships.

In the inbreaking kingdom, relationships are called to be rightly aligned. When we relate to others in ways that are holy and just, we find perfection: a whole and complete reflection of God's heart. In the Trinity, God is one: pure, holy love in three persons. This is the kingdom wholeness we are called to reflect!

—*CARLA SUNBERG*

TODAY

Pray over your calling to live in anointed, just relationship with others.

THE LIVELY SPIRIT OF HOLY LOVE

And who through the Spirit of holiness was appointed the Son of God
in power by his resurrection from the dead: Jesus Christ our Lord. (Rom. 1:4)

Have you allowed faulty concepts of dead or sour holiness to distract you so deeply you've lost your zeal to live in the Spirit of holiness found in Christ? This would be a tragic loss! The promise of genuine holiness is powerful and transformational—exactly what our world needs today. Most people would probably be shocked to discover what true holiness looks like.

This is the holy calling of every follower of Jesus Christ: we are invited into the Spirit of holiness, life in Jesus Christ. We are called to be transformed into the likeness of Jesus, so that his nature of holy love will flow through every one of us. You and I are called to live in the holiness of Christ through the lively power of the Holy Spirit. Holiness does not dull us or deaden our fervor; it's not a legalistic path for a few strict people. It is the enlivening way of Christ through the creative power of the Spirit. It is for all God's people, everywhere, always. We are all called to be lively like Jesus; a holy, loving people.

PRAYER

Lord, help my sisters to lean into your lively Spirit of holy love.
May we move forward in your boldness through resurrection power,
embracing your Spirit and loving our world. Amen.

REV. DR. CARLA SUNBERG

is General Superintendent of the Church of the Nazarene. She previously served
as a pastor and missionary, and president of Wesleyan Holiness
Women Clergy and Nazarene Theological Seminary.

BORN AGAIN THROUGH BAPTISM

Jesus replied, "Very truly I tell you, no one can see
the kingdom of God unless they are born again." (John 3:3)

My journey to pastoral ministry took place alongside my journey to motherhood, and many special pastoral moments happened while I was pregnant. I loved preaching, serving Communion, counseling, and praying for the congregation— with a belly. But perhaps my favorite pastoral duty to perform while pregnant was baptism.

Baptism is a means of God's grace, a way for us to experience God in our lives. Baptism is our spiritual rebirth, through which God makes us into new creations, bringing us into the family of God.

As a pregnant pastor, it was impossible for me to ignore the innately feminine nature of baptism. I was a woman preparing to birth new life into the world and, at the same time, I was a pastor ushering people through their spiritual rebirth in Jesus Christ. As a new creation was forming in my womb, I guided those whom God was making into new creations.

Whether or not you ever physically give birth, as a woman, you bear the image of the God who calls the world to be born again. When you baptize someone into the family of God, that act highlights the motherliness of God's mission in the world and gives the Church a special glimpse into elements of God we associate with the femininity of God. In baptism, you partner with God in the motherly work of making all things new.

—KATE WALLACE NUNNELEY

TODAY

Remember your baptism; baptize, showing the
world the mothering power of God.

COMMUNION AS SPIRITUAL FOOD

While they were eating, Jesus took bread, and when he had given thanks, he broke it and gave it to his disciples, saying, "Take and eat; this is my body." (Matt. 26:26)

Receiving Holy Communion from a woman forever changed my understanding of the Lord's Table. Growing up, male pastors and elders usually presided over the Table. Scripture was read and Jesus' words were spoken, but if I'm honest, Communion wasn't significant for me.

But when a woman broke the bread and said those precious words, "This is my body, take and eat," Jesus spoke to me anew.

The story of Jesus begins with Mary bringing the body and blood of Jesus into the world. In a sense, she was the first to preside over the Table, the first to offer those holy elements to humanity. Although not all the events of that first night are recorded in scripture, after she had given birth, I can imagine Mary whispering something similar to her baby as she fed him: "This is my body, take and eat." When a biological mother gives birth to a child, she sometimes attempts to give life through the ongoing sustenance from her own body. She offers herself so they might live.

Jesus' words at the Last Supper speak to his body broken and blood shed on the cross, yes. But they also remind us of a birthing mother offering all she is to her child, nourishing from her own body. Communion not only reminds us of Jesus' death; it is a picture of the life Jesus continues to give us as children of God.

—KATE WALLACE NUNNELEY

TODAY

Consider Communion; come to the Table, receiving the
sustenance God has for you.

PROCLAIMING EMBODIED GRACE

Then God said, "Let us make humankind in our image, according to our likeness."
(Gen. 1:26 NRSV)

Our God is triune—three in one, experiencing holy fellowship within the diversity of the Trinity. Humanity wouldn't have reflected this holy fellowship if just one being had been created. So God created humanity "in our image," not as one person, but as a whole human community, with fellowship and partnership between the genders.

And yet, in the majority of churches, that is what leadership looks like—men alone. Despite being created for diverse fellowship, many Christians insist that Church leadership should be solely male. This has left the Church anemic. No, each human bears the full image. Otherwise, only married folks would be imago dei.

As a female pastor, you bring something to the Church that has been missing for far too long. You bring a different perspective, a different voice, a different reflection of the image of God. A friend once told me that when women preach, we preach two messages: one verbal and one nonverbal. We verbally preach the message we have prepared, and we preach nonverbally simply by being a woman in the pulpit.

The Church needs your scriptural edification and the image of God you bring to the platform. When you preach, teach, baptize, and preside over Holy Communion, you call the Church back to the fellowship we were created to be.

—KATE WALLACE NUNNELEY

TODAY

Pastor not in spite of your femininity, but because of it.

READY GRACE: MEETING GOD IN PRAYER

"This, then, is how you should pray:
'Our Father in heaven, hallowed be your name.'" (Matt. 6:9)

Most days I work from my favorite coffee shop. My husband and our eighteen-month-old son often visit me there. Frequently I'm working at my table when I hear a little voice say, "Mama?" I look up to see Jonathan nervously standing in the doorway. So I crouch down with my arms open, and when his little eyes catch mine, his face lights up and he yells, "Mama," and runs full speed into my arms.

Jonathan is young. He doesn't yet know who he is. But in that moment he knows the only thing that truly matters: I am his mama, he is my son, and that is enough.

For leaders, it's easy to fall into the trap of finding our identity in our work and thinking of God as our boss. Jesus teaches us to address God not as boss, judge, or king, but as "Father," reminding us that first and foremost, God is our loving parent, and we are God's children. When we pray, we can walk into the throne room of God the way Jonathan walks into that coffee shop—with the audacity of a child running into outstretched arms!

When you do, surely you will find God kneeling down, arms open, ready to enfold you in love, reminding you of the only thing that truly matters: God is your loving parent, you are God's child, and that is enough.

—KATE WALLACE NUNNELEY

TODAY

Run into the arms of God; remember who you truly are.

THE PROMISE IN FASTING DISCOURAGEMENT

For some days I mourned and fasted and prayed
before the God of heaven. (Neh. 1:4)

In the Wesleyan tradition, fasting is about making space in our lives so that we become more aware of the presence of God. In other words, fasting isn't only about what you take out of your life but what you do with that space when it's been cleared.

As women who pastor, we face a lot of criticism. Many do not believe we should be pastoring at all. Even many who say they are supportive do not shy away from telling us exactly what they think about us—our hair, our clothes, the pitch of our voice. It takes a lot of energy just to block out those voices and get on with the mission.

What would happen if we turned that pivot into a spiritual practice? What might happen if we fasted discouragement? What if we give up those voices that criticize us for being who God made us to be and doing what God called us to do? What if we let go of all those comments we hold on to, those nasty words that stick with us, burning them as a fragrant offering to God?

And what if we filled the space left behind with God's promises: reading and rereading them until they simply become part of who we are?

I don't think it would be easy; fasting never is. But perhaps you and I would feel the presence of God in new ways.

—KATE WALLACE NUNNELEY

 TODAY

Seize moments to fast discouragement and
receive promises; see what God does.

THE GRACE OF PREACHING SCRIPTURE

She said to them, "This is what the LORD,
the God of Israel, says: . . ." (2 Kings 22:15; 2 Chron. 34:23)

Since ancient times, God has called women to use their voices for the betterment of God's people—to call God's people back to justice, truth, holiness: the ways of God.

This is what God does with Huldah. In a sea of male voices—male priests, male scholars, male prophets—God uses the voice of a woman to speak what the men had not. Huldah knows God and uses her voice to bring others back to Him.

Wesleyans affirm that searching scripture is a means of God's grace, a way for us to experience the transforming presence of God in our lives. Never have I found this to be more true than when I am preaching what I have learned in the scriptures. When I use my female voice to preach what God has shown me in God's Word, it is a special means of grace; perhaps only those who know what it's like to be silenced can understand.

As women pastors, we know what it's like to have our voices silenced, feared, and questioned. Even though we have been called to preach to a world in need, in our darkest moments, discouragement can breed doubt.

When you find yourself in that place, let the stories of women like Huldah, Deborah, Anna, Mary, Priscilla, and so many others encourage you. Like them, you have been called by God to use your voice.

—KATE WALLACE NUNNELEY

TODAY

Preach the Word, and let it be a special means of grace for you.

THE GRACE OF DIGNITY: GO AND DO

I thank my God every time I remember you. In all my prayers for all of you,
I always pray with joy because of your partnership in the gospel. (Phil. 1:3–5)

Women, your worth and dignity are not determined by how well you fit into someone's definition of "biblical womanhood." They aren't determined by getting married, having kids, staying cooperatively quiet, or being submissive.

Women, your worth and dignity were determined the moment you were created in the image of the living God; your place in the kingdom was secured the moment your sin was nailed to the cross and defeated by the risen Christ.

Women, your worth and dignity are not things to be debated, because they are not things that can be taken away, lost, or earned. They simply are.

Women, you have been called to lead God's Church. So go and do. Preach the gospel, lead God's people, invite others to the Table, baptize, pray, marry, bury, counsel, lead.

You bear God's image. An image that for far too long has been kept from pulpits, platforms, and presiding at the Table.

Your voice is power. Your presence, a gift.

Women, your partnership in the gospel brings me such joy—and I thank God every time I remember you.

PRAYER

Mothering God, you formed and called us. Let our ministries be a means
of grace for us, that we might feel your presence as we baptize,
break bread, pray, fast, and preach in the fellowship of believers. Amen.

REV. KATE WALLACE NUNNELEY
is an ordained pastor in the Free Methodist Church and cofounder
of The Junia Project, a ministry that teaches biblical equality,
equips women, and resources the Church.

FIRST THINGS FIRST

We know and rely on the love God has for us. God is love.
Whoever lives in love lives in God, and God in them. (1 John 4:16)

Pastors. Housewives. Professionals. Retirees. College students. I've served all types of women in the context of spiritual freedom ministry. More often than not, there comes a beautiful and pivotal moment in which someone realizes she has a faulty perception not just of who she is but who God is. I can't begin to count the times I've had the honor of watching the Holy Spirit reveal the heart of God to these women—God's heart for each one as an individual. They come knowing about Jesus but leave knowing him on a personal level; they leave convinced of God's love.

God is love. Old Testament and New Testament alike, that is who God is. God doesn't change. God doesn't have momentary lapses of character or act in unloving ways. Everything God does is from a foundation of love, because that's the nature of the Trinity. God doesn't just possess love, God *is* love. When God seems silent, he is love. When God doesn't make sense, he is love. When God gives and takes away, he is love. Until you grasp that fundamental truth of God's very nature of creative, infinite love, you won't fully recognize your own identity.

Have you recently spent time intentionally focusing on God's character and attributes? *Agape* love is God's very nature and being. Ask God to give you a new perspective on his love for you, then actively anticipate seeing God's love today.

—TERRA PENNINGA

TODAY

Focus on God's deep love for *you*, not just for those around you.

WE ARE GOD'S

Know that the LORD is God. It is he who made us, and we are his. (Ps. 100:3)

Let's say it together: "God is already pleased with me!" As competent women who have been called into ministry, this can be a difficult truth for us to walk in. In the spirit of honesty, there have been times I've considered myself to be God's "employee of the month." I've believed the Father of Lies, who tells me that if I slow down and rest, the kingdom of God is going to fall apart. In those moments, how much more proud could I be in my thinking?

God has not created us to be his hired hands or assistant managers. In the Sermon on the Mount, Jesus echoes Psalm 100 and assures his listeners that they don't have to do anything to earn God's love or affection. The birds of the air don't make an effort to earn God's affection, but God is pleased with them regardless of their performance. The birds don't find their identity in how productive they are throughout the year or how well their nest is built. They simply are. The birds are his, and so are we.

When was the last time you stopped trying to perform? When was the last time that you didn't assess yourself on church attendance statistics, sermon quality, a parenting faux pas, or other successes or failures? I challenge you to find a few moments today to sit and be still. Remember that you are God's, and God is pleased with you.

—TERRA PENNINGA

TODAY

Quiet yourself and trust that you don't have to earn God's affection.

IN GOD'S IMAGE

So God created humankind in his image, in the image of God he
created them; male and female he created them. (Gen. 1:27 NRSV)

Hi. My name is Terra and I'm a wife, mom, daughter, sister, friend, counselor, mentor, volunteer, pastor, and neighbor. Have you ever thought about how many ways you can identify yourself? Have you ever entertained a sinful attitude about the things you've accomplished or the sinful attitude of shame when you don't live up to your own expectations?

It's in those moments I'm thankful my identity isn't about me at all. My identity is about the One in whose image I'm made. I have been created in God's image, and it's God's Spirit that dwells within me so that I may reflect Christ. It's a comfort to know I don't have to work harder or exhaust myself by trying to be the best pastor or mom or friend on the planet. Instead, I can rest in my identity of being created in the image of God, trust that God's pleased with me, and allow Christ to live through me.

The next time you are tempted to find your identity in how many or how few roles you have, remember your identity isn't found there. Your identity isn't even found in how "successful" you are in those roles. You have been created in the likeness of the God of the universe. Rest in the One who gives you your identity. Let all of that unnecessary striving melt away as you look to God who made you in his own likeness.

—TERRA PENNINGA

TODAY

Stop striving and let God live through you.

HOLY AND BLAMELESS

For he chose us in him before the creation of the world to be
holy and blameless in his sight. (Eph. 1:4)

Recently, I visited my dear friend. She is ninety-three years old, and her body is beginning to fail. By the time you read this, she will have seen Jesus face-to-face. During my visit, my friend kept saying she didn't deserve a hospital visit from me. I finally asked, "Why do you think so poorly of yourself?" She responded quickly, "I'm just me. I get jealous of others. I have pride in things I've accomplished. I don't think I'll ever be pleased with myself." I was taken aback by her response, then asked if she knew that God was pleased with her. Her silence indicated she wasn't convinced of God's approval.

I was deeply saddened that a woman who spent the majority of her life as a missionary telling others about Jesus wouldn't know the deep love of the Father for her. She didn't feel the truth that she was chosen before the creation of the world to be holy and blameless. She wasn't fully convinced of her identity.

I'd venture to say we've all examined and judged ourselves like this. We're so aware of our own brokenness that we forget what God says about who we are. God sees us as holy and blameless! When you start to feel displeased with yourself, remember that God's truth and your identity cannot be taken from you.

—TERRA PENNINGA

TODAY

Say aloud, "I am holy and blameless in Christ."

IN THE IMAGE OF ELOHIM

Then God said, "Let us make humankind in our image,
according to our likeness." (Gen. 1:26 NRSV)

The phrase "divide and conquer" is a cliché because it's such an effective battle strategy. And I humbly admit that I compare myself to you. Maybe you're prettier. More eloquent. More passionate. More effective. More _____ (fill in the blank). I take the enemy's bait, plain and simple. But when I compare, I minimize the opportunity to have authentic relationships. I allow the enemy to divide and conquer. When I close myself off to relationships, I am forgetting that I am made in the image of God.

Father, Son, and Spirit. God, in God's very self, is a relationship—Trinity, three in one. That's God's identity; that's who God is. Scripture makes it clear that the persons of the Trinity enliven each other. The Father sends the Holy Spirit. The Holy Spirit elevates Jesus. Jesus honors the Father. That is the image in which we are made!

My friend, as one who has been made in God's image, you have been made for relationship—not the kind of relationship that exists on the surface, comparing with others, but the kind of relationship that loves deeply, builds others up, and honors the Lord with every interaction. Doing this moves us away from the enemy's plan and aligns us with God's purposes!

—TERRA PENNINGA

TODAY

Confess and repent of comparison;
pursue relationships that reflect *Elohim*'s image.

IDENTIFIED BY SURRENDER

Rather, he made himself nothing by taking the very nature
of a servant, being made in human likeness. (Phil. 2:7)

To love control, you need only be human. Have you ever tried to control a situation that you knew was impossible to control? But something inside you was compelled to try to orchestrate and commandeer all the variables so that you would experience a predictable, controlled outcome. I assume some of you are nodding your head in ardent agreement.

Today's verse from Philippians comes in the larger context of Jesus' mindset of servanthood and humility. We pursue Christlikeness and Jesus chose the identity of a servant. He chose to walk in an identity of entire sanctification. Every act of Jesus was an act of surrender to the Father. In Genesis, we read that humanity was made in God's likeness. And now in Philippians we read that Jesus turned everything on its head, choosing to be made in human likeness. As a human, Jesus gives an example of surrender and sanctification that is possible for all of us. He relinquished all control into the hands of the Father.

Is the Spirit inside of you drawing you to a deeper level of surrender? Jesus surrendered the trajectory of his entire life to embody the sacrificial love of the Trinity. This is what entire sanctification looks like. How would your daily life change if sanctification wasn't a goal but an identity that can't be taken from you? Would you bravely surrender and relinquish control into the hands of Christ?

—TERRA PENNINGA

TODAY

Identify one area you've tried to control; surrender it to God.

OUR IDENTITY OF UNITY

I have given them the glory that you gave me,
that they may be one as we are one. (John 17:22)

As Christians, we believe we are made in the image of God. We believe our personal identity is found in who Jesus Christ is. But what do we believe about our identity as the Body of Christ?

Jesus' prayer for you and me isn't a prayer of individual identity; it's a prayer of corporate identity. Jesus prays that we would be one just like the Father, Son, and Spirit are one. This unity isn't a polite tolerance of one another; it's a unity that honors, builds up, and loves one another. It's only when we walk in this identity of unity that the world will be convinced of the deep love Christ has for them.

We can embrace our individual identity of being surrendered, holy, blameless, and sanctified. But what might happen if we walk in our individual identity while simultaneously fastening ourselves to a larger identity of unity as a body of believers? What if the Body of Christ were one, just as the Father, Son, and Spirit are one? What if.

PRAYER

Jesus, I want to be convinced of who you are, who I am,
and how I can live my life in a way that honors you.
Help me to do this by the power of your Holy Spirit. Amen.

REV. TERRA PENNINGA

has served in ministry for twenty-one years, including time working with
Thirteenth Tribe Ministries and Branch Adventures, a Christian camp for kids.
She is passionate about praying scripture and encouraging others
in their spiritual freedom. She and her husband live in
central Michigan with their two children.

WHO DO YOU SEE?

Then the righteous will answer him, "Lord, when did we see you hungry and feed you, or thirsty and give you something to drink?" (Matt. 25:37)

"Y'all see her? Y'all see me? When you see her, you see me. When you see me, you see her. Period. Don't play with my best friend!" A recording of a woman's voice speaking these words became the basis for a viral social media challenge during the COVID-19 pandemic. People posted videos to the TikTok app acting out the recorded words with their best friends and telling the world that seeing one of them was seeing both of them. The message was clear—how you treat my best friend is how you treat me.

In the parable of the sheep and goats, the righteous wondered aloud: when did we see Jesus hungry, thirsty, unclothed, a stranger, a prisoner, or sick and meet his needs? Likewise, the unjust wondered: when did we see Jesus and not meet his needs? Jesus' response might be reworded for the TikTok generation: "When you saw them, you saw me. When you met their need, you met my need. They are made in my image. Period. Don't play with the least of these."

The unjust meet human needs based on who they deem to be "human enough." But the righteous see the humanity—the image of God—in each individual without qualification, and do their part to effect justice: to make whole. Who do you see?

—KEISHA I. PATRICK

See God's image in marginalized people and communities;
act so they receive justice.

JUST WATER

I am making a way in the wilderness and streams in the wasteland. (Isa. 43:19)

In 2014, local government leaders changed the source of water for Flint, Michigan, residents to address a budget crisis. Lead-filled water began to flow from city pipes into the homes of Flint's poorest residents and their children's bloodstreams because unjust leaders prioritized money over the lives of people living in a marginalized community. When the news hit headlines, people from all over the country began donating bottled water to Flint. Despite the donations, many residents were still subjected to lead-filled water in their homes until at least 2019. Charitable acts could not fix the broken system.

When the Israelites found themselves in a desert place experiencing oppression under Babylonian rule, God promised to deliver them. A new ecosystem would revive what was then wilderness and wasteland through God-placed pathways and streams. The oppressor's actions would be deconstructed, and God's people would have a continual source of life-giving water. No more desert.

The long-term consequences of the Flint water crisis are yet to be seen. We must work to affirm the humanity of marginalized people, transform unjust systems, and revive oppressed communities. Until then, charitable actions will simply be Band-Aids attempting to cover wounds without salve for healing. The Rev. Dr. Martin Luther King Jr. stated: "Philanthropy is commendable, but it must not cause the philanthropist to overlook the circumstances of economic injustice which make philanthropy necessary."

—KEISHA I. PATRICK

TODAY

Recognize and dismantle systems of oppression so revival can flood the land.

FOR ALL NATiONS

And as he taught them, he said, "Is it not written:
'My house will be called a house of prayer for all nations'?" (Mark 11:17)

Americans seem to unite around our love for baseball. In my hometown of St. Louis, there's nothing we collectively agree on more than our love for the St. Louis Cardinals. But while my grandfather loved baseball, he was not a Cardinals fan. He migrated to St. Louis to escape the Jim Crow South. Still, he found that the hometown team was among the slowest in the league to integrate its players. Additionally, the team excluded his wife—my grandmother—from participating in Women's Day at the ballpark because she was Black. My grandfather had escaped the South but had not escaped oppression. Even after the times forced the Cardinals to change, my grandfather could not get past the unjust, dehumanizing principles the team held tightly for too long.

Jesus had righteous anger over the injustice he observed when he entered the temple. Non-Jews were being excluded from worship and poor people were being exploited for financial gain. God intended for people from any and all nationalities, ethnicities, and racial backgrounds to worship God at the temple. Jesus acted out in rebuke to the injustice he observed, because he knew that oppression blocked people from connecting with and worshiping God.

Whether in sports, in our houses of worship, or in any other part of society, we must rebuke injustice; it dehumanizes people created in God's image.

—KEISHA I. PATRICK

TODAY

Rebuke injustice; be openhearted toward those who are unlike you.

MOTHERS' LIVES MATTER

As she breathed her last—for she was dying—she named her son
Ben-Oni. But his father named him Benjamin. (Gen. 35:18)

"I want to go to heaven to see my mommy," four-year-old Soleil said to her grandmother. Soleil's mom, Dr. Shalon Irving, had collapsed at home and died in 2017, just three weeks after Soleil was born. Shalon was an epidemiologist with the CDC; her doctor had been dismissive of her repeated complaint of pain, that something was wrong. America has the highest rate of maternal and infant mortality in the industrialized world. For Black women and babies, the mortality rate is three to four times higher than for White women and babies. Studies show doctors are often dismissive of Black women's statements of symptoms. Even world-famous tennis star Serena Williams experienced dangerous medical dismissiveness that almost cost the professional athlete her life after giving birth. Can Christians profess pro-life values if the solvable crises of maternal and infant mortality are dismissed or ignored?

Like Soleil, Joseph and his brother Benjamin lost their mother Rachel from childbirth-related complications. Genesis records that Rachel breathed her last after giving birth to Benjamin. Imagine how different Joseph's life could have been if his mother had lived. Perhaps she would have helped him discern his brothers' envy. Maybe Joseph wouldn't have ended up in a pit. Perhaps maternal intuition would have hinted to Rachel that Joseph was still alive.

If we value women, will we not experience righteous anger over the maternal and infant mortality crises and their disproportionate impact on people of color? No child should grow up not having her mother; no child should grow up with the burden of knowing that his mother died giving birth to him.

—KEISHA I. PATRICK

TODAY

Grieve preventable death; advocate for medical equity
to reduce maternal and infant mortality.

LET THE MUSIC PLAY

But he wanted to justify himself, so he asked Jesus,
"And who is my neighbor?" (Luke 10:29)

The unique sounds of go-go music flow through Washington, DC, culture. For twenty-four years, a small business owner blasted go-go into the streets of a DC neighborhood from his store's speakers. The city's natives loved it! Then, a new demographic of neighbors submitted noise complaints to the police and threatened lawsuits, forcing the store to mute the go-go. The new neighbors rejected DC culture and, implicitly, the city's natives. But DC natives protested through live concerts and the social media campaign #dontmuteDC until the music was allowed to play again. The grassroots #dontmuteDC movement resulted in the city council designating go-go as the city's official music as well as the launch of an annual DC Natives Day.

When Jesus confirmed that eternal life hinges on both our love for God and for our neighbor, he essentially stated that no neighbor is to be muted. No justification exists for excluding any neighbor. Jesus illustrated this through a piercing parable in which the most unlikely person proved to be the truest neighbor.

Our world categorizes us based on arbitrary factors that have no eternal significance. Still, the factors are largely determinative of where and with whom we live, work, and worship and of who can access wealth and resources. If we are not careful, we will unwittingly exclude our truest neighbors based on false beliefs that our arbitrary factors make us right, and their arbitrary factors make them wrong.

—KEISHA I. PATRICK

TODAY

Respect and find joy in all our neighbors as God's image bearers.

NO TIME TO JUDGE

But a Samaritan, as he traveled, came where the man was;
and when he saw him, he took pity on him. (Luke 10:33)

After a Minneapolis police officer killed George Floyd in 2020, protests took place worldwide. During a London Black Lives Matter gathering, protestor Patrick Hutchinson noticed an injured counter-protestor lying in the fetal position, surrounded by a crowd. Concerned the counter-protestor's life was in danger, Hutchinson picked up the injured man, carrying him to safety. Hutchinson told BBC News: "I wasn't thinking. I was just thinking of a human being on the floor. . . . I had no other thoughts in my mind apart from getting to safety." Recalling the death of George Floyd, Hutchinson told another news outlet that Floyd would still be alive if other officers on the scene had intervened.

In Jesus' parable, Jesus demonstrated that Jewish lives matter in order to prove that Samaritan lives matter, too. Samaritans were enemies of the Jews, of a different religion and ethnicity. After two Jewish leaders passed by a Jewish man lying on the ground half-dead, a Samaritan came along and took pity. The Samaritan didn't make judgments about how the man ended up in such a predicament or the man's worthiness to be made whole. The Samaritan simply recognized the man's humanity, acting with empathy. Jesus instructed his listeners to do likewise.

When a person or community is in dire need, is it tempting to assume? To deny help, wondering if other people are worthy of helping? The only determination for worthiness that Christians are called to consider is whether the person bears the image of God.

—KEISHA I. PATRICK

TODAY

Act quickly and without judgment when human life is in need.

LIBERATING COURAGE

The LORD is my light and my salvation—whom shall I fear? (Ps. 27:1)

With the Confederate flag in hand, Bree Newsome recited Psalm 27 as she descended the flagpole on the grounds of the South Carolina Capitol on June 27, 2015. Politicians had discussed but taken no action to remove the flag, a symbol of hatred and oppression that taunted African Americans. The funerals of nine Black churchgoers massacred at Mother Emanuel AME by a White supremacist had begun, and mourners still had to behold the hateful symbol that had emboldened the murderer. James Tyson stood at the flagpole's base, supporting Bree and possibly preventing an unfortunate police encounter. Bree was arrested as well as James, Bree's accomplice in fighting for justice.

Often, when Jesus performed miracles liberating people from oppression, others sought to have him arrested and killed. Luke 4 records that shortly after Jesus announced his mission to proclaim justice for the poor, incarcerated, blind, and oppressed, people wanted to kill him. But Jesus courageously continued his mission until the government murdered him.

We are called to be accomplices to Jesus' mission to set the oppressed free. With the Lord as our light and salvation, we have nobody to fear.

PRAYER

God, help me to see and honor your image in each person and community of persons. Grant me courage to be an accomplice in your liberation mission to set the oppressed free in body and soul.

REV. KEISHA I. PATRICK, ESQ.

is the youth and young adult pastor at Third Street Church of God in Washington, DC and is a member of the ministries council for the Church of God (Anderson) [USA]. She practices law for a federal agency. She loves to travel, especially overseas. She is #singleaunting (a.k.a. parenting) her nephew Karsten, who is in college.

CALLED TOWARD CHRIST

FILLING UP ON GOOD THINGS

But when you fast, put oil on your head and wash your face,
so that it will not be obvious to others. (Matt. 6:17–18)

Dieting fads have caused so many issues for women of all ages; women in the church are not exempt. Women leaders, pastors, and preachers are not exempt. We look at our bodies and compare them to others: on social media, in commercials, even other women we personally encounter. From a very young age, we are cued to think our bodies are somehow deficient and that there is a perfect body.

Sadly, this was how I first encountered the practice of fasting: temporarily abstaining from eating food, many of the foods I enjoyed, because eating them would somehow make me not "good enough." In my relationship with Christ, as I began to encounter him in my everyday life, I realized that Christ wanted to be in relationship with me. That profoundly changed the way I approached fasting. Rather than fast to avoid certain foods so I could somehow make the outside better, I fasted to strengthen and beautify my inward life.

Moses fasted forty days. The prophets, disciples, and Jesus fasted. This had everything to do with their relationship to God rather than devaluing their physical bodies. Fasting changes us from the inside, drawing us nearer to the Lord. Food and other things are moved out of the way, making space for filling up on the good things of God. What can you choose to fast from to make room for the abundance of Christ?

—NATALIE GIDNEY

TODAY

Choose a period of time to fast and spend time with God.

GENEROUS PRAYER

But I tell you, love your enemies and pray for those who persecute you. (Matt. 5:44)

Women in ministry have an uphill battle to fight. The internet trolls are everywhere, telling women what they can and cannot do, especially in the leadership of the church. This should not be—especially in holiness denominations that believe (on paper anyway) that there is equality for women in ministry.

The prophet Joel prophesied that women would receive the Spirit and prophesy, yet there are many who would tell us to be quiet, or that our callings are not valid, or in the worst cases, that we are blasphemous. The number of women who have been silenced and turned away from following their calling is a tragedy to the kingdom of God.

For those who have continued to trek the uphill battle, for those who have broken through the stained-glass ceiling, and for those who have shattered it: God sees you, God celebrates you, and the Holy Spirit continues to anoint and be with you.

The best thing women preachers, leaders, and teachers can do for those who oppose their calling is to pray for them. Pray they will be convicted of the lies they are believing and spreading; pray for the healing of their hearts; pray for them to clearly see the truth of the Word of God. Prayer changes things. Prayer changes us. Through prayer, we encounter the Holy One who can change even the most hardened and calloused heart.

—NATALIE GIDNEY

TODAY

Pray by name for those who oppose your calling.

GROW DEEP ROOTS

I meditate on your precepts and consider your ways. (Ps. 119:15)

"If you know how to worry, you know how to meditate." This popular idea has taken me by surprise at times. When you consider the meaning of worry, it is simply thinking about something over and over again from a negative angle. Meditation is the practice of dwelling on things but without the negative slant. At times, meditation has been looked at by some Christians with hostility when it is approached solely as a fad that New Age practitioners teach. However, when we consider the basic meaning of meditation and its practice throughout church history—putting scripture and the attributes of our triune God at the center—meditation can be a game changer in our spiritual habits.

My great-grandmother kept her Bible open on her kitchen table and never ate without referring to specific psalms or proverbs each day. She would read it and drink her tea and read it again and again throughout the day. Her intentionality speaks to me now more than ever, in ways I couldn't see when I was young. Taking a verse and ruminating on it—rolling it over and over—settles it in the heart in deep and profound ways that are transformative.

As a woman who preaches, teaches, and leads, is meditating on scripture a practice in your spiritual life? The psalmists often bring up meditation, as do some of the prophets; Jesus modeled it. If it was important for them, we should take note and do likewise.

—NATALIE GIDNEY

TODAY

Write a scripture verse and meditate on it through the day.

SACRED STILLNESS

Tremble and do not sin; when you are on your beds,
search your hearts and be silent. (Ps. 4:4)

For the hearing, silence can be frightening to some, comforting to others. In the "daily grind" of a woman leader's life, audible noise or the fast pace of busyness are common. We do not need to make time for loud activity or full schedules; they organically happen. Stillness, on the other hand—whether physical silence or halted activity—is a discipline for which we must deliberately carve out time and space, if we are to benefit from it.

When I began spending time in stillness or silence, it was extremely difficult. I would shift and sigh. The stillness itself seemed uncomfortable. I wondered how I would be able to sense anything in a space so still. I am an extrovert, usually happy to interact with multiple people, sometimes while "multitasking"—though this is not always a good thing.

Something we desperately need happens in our spirits in the midst of stillness. As I learn to spend time in physical silence or stilled activity, I begin to understand why some people take vows of silence or why some monasteries are built away from busy town squares. There can be holy space in stillness. There is room for awe, reverence, and peace that comes from sitting undistracted, away from overstimulation, in the presence of the Lord. Often, we find it easy to be busy, speaking or expressing ourselves, desperately wanting to be understood or heard. There is a peaceful shift within when being peaceful and still informs our interactions with others.

—NATALIE GIDNEY

TODAY

Sit, walk, or hike in stillness with the Lord.

FREEDOM THROUGH CONFESSION

If we confess our sins, he is faithful and just and will forgive us our sins
and purify us from all unrighteousness. (1 John 1:9)

We all struggle. There are temptations in each of our lives. Sometimes you and I make the wrong choice, entering a place we wish we hadn't gone, doing things we wish we hadn't done. Thankfully, we have an advocate in Jesus, who is waiting for us to come to him. Each time we approach Christ, he is faithful to forgive.

At different times, I have struggled with shame and guilt. Sometimes it feels like I will never be free, but that is simply not true. I take my sin to Christ, confess where I have fallen short, and receive his forgiveness, healing, and restoration. When the enemy of my soul reminds me of the past and tries to trap me in shame, I take it to the Father, who reminds me gently, "Daughter, you have been forgiven."

Some people never let you forget your mistakes. If you confide something to someone untrustworthy, they may throw it in your face. But in Jesus, we have an advocate who throws our sins as far away as the east is from the west, into the depths of the sea, never again reminding us. If you give Christ full access to your life, he is faithful to bring transformative change through the Holy Spirit in you, empowering you to refuse temptation and be holy—and joyful—as he is holy and joyful.

—NATALIE GIDNEY

TODAY

Consider your life and confess any sin that is hindering you.

HOLY REST

For anyone who enters God's rest also rests from their works,
just as God did from his. (Heb. 4:10)

When my girls were small, it was easy to realize the importance of rest in their lives. Sleepless nights meant long, tiring days with cranky children. Knowing this, I scheduled early bedtimes and worked out rhythms for quieting them with a bedtime routine of baths, stories, and prayer, which—most often—led to sleep. Rest was vital for their growth and well-being.

For a time, I had to step away from ministry due to burnout. I had overextended myself continually for ten years, both personally and professionally. Rest is a spiritual discipline that should become part of our daily spiritual habits; beyond that, taking a Sabbath break is vital. After creating the world, God took a day to rest. A Sabbath rest means taking a full twenty-four hours from doing work once a week.

Here in my own North American work culture, rest is sometimes seen as indulgent, portrayed as lazy or unproductive. But rest can be the most productive thing you do for yourself and those around you. Failing to prioritize rest can make us like unruly children who haven't had enough sleep. Eventually, it will show in our interactions with other people, our spiritual lives, and even our physical health. Are you feeling like an exhausted or unruly child?

—NATALIE GIDNEY

TODAY

Pursue rest or a sabbatical—or make one available to a colleague.

A TIME TO CELEBRATE

That each of them may eat and drink, and find satisfaction
in all their toil—this is the gift of God. (Eccl. 3:13)

Almost five months to the day after I had last preached, I preached to a camera in an empty sanctuary. It felt great. After burning out, I had stepped away to rest. Now, the passion and purpose I had before returned in full clarity. Though I was alone, the presence of the Holy Spirit was thick; I sensed his powerful anointing.

I left for my commute home, ecstatic. It was time to celebrate what God had done in my spirit during the break. I reflected on the truth: Jesus restores, redeems, heals; Jesus came to seek and save the lost, hurting, and broken; Jesus had done all of it for me.

I was so excited I decided to truly celebrate, stopping at my favorite coffee shop for my favorite sandwich and iced latte, smiling as the barista passed them to me. I headed to the beach to remember all Christ had done in me and to celebrate what God would continue to do through me. There is something special and sacred about celebrating the good things God does in our lives!

PRAYER

God, thank you for the gift of rest. In rest, we demonstrate our dependence
on you. Help us receive the holy rest you call us to. Renew our spirits
so we can celebrate our calling, finding joy in you. Amen.

REV. NATALIE GIDNEY
serves as assistant pastor of discipleship at a Wesleyan church in
Weymouth, Novia Scotia, Canada, and on the communications team of
Wesleyan Holiness Women Clergy. She has authored four books on discipleship,
and enjoys walking on the beach, reading, and cooking. She was called into ministry
at age 39 and started her ministry journey at age 40. She has three children.

CREATOR

God saw all that he had made, and it was very good. (Gen. 1:31)

Are you ever hard on yourself? Over time, I began to notice that I tend to be harder on myself than others are toward me. Frequently, I have high expectations. But this is not unique to me; it is something I see in those around me as well.

Is it possible that you have become your own worst critic? It is easy to tear myself down and break my own spirit, focusing on the negative rather than the good. It is tempting to see my flaws or allow negative thoughts to dominate my perspective.

But when God created, it was good. We learn this from the very first verses of the Bible, and that theme continues throughout scripture. God continues to create and re-create, and what God has made is good.

God has made each one of us; God formed us and created us unique and special. Every single human being is beautiful. If my creator God can see me and call me good, what right do I have to speak so negatively to myself? What right do I have to dwell on my flaws? If God can call me good, I need to receive this truth and dwell in it. Imagine with me our God creating from love and calling it "good." You are an important part of God's beautiful creation. Hear this truth: you are good.

—SHANNON L. NEW SPANGLER

TODAY

Write three good things God created you to be.

PROVIDER

And my God will meet all your needs according to the
riches of his glory in Christ Jesus. (Phil. 4:19)

After the exodus from Egypt, the Israelites found themselves in the desert. They were being led through an unknown wilderness and were probably scared. As the people became hungry, they began to get angry. They questioned why Moses and Aaron brought them out of Egypt only to have them starve to death in the wilderness. But this was not the plan; the Lord is a provider. When God saw that the people were hungry, he spoke to Moses and said that manna would be sent, enough for each day. And that is exactly what God did: he sent manna daily, providing for their needs.

There are many moments in life that require provision from God, places where we need him to step in—perhaps a question to be answered or a need to be met. While we may not get the answer we think is best, we can be certain from the witness of scripture that God is a provider. You and I are never left alone to fend for ourselves; God is *Yaweh-Jireh* (which means "the Lord will provide").

When I look over my life, it is easy to see those places where God stepped in and provided for my needs, even when provision didn't look like I expected. We can trust that God will provide. Are you ready to lean into the truth of that promise?

—SHANNON L. NEW SPANGLER

TODAY

Write what God has provided for you this week.

SAVIOR

"She will give birth to a son, and you are to give him the name Jesus,
because he will save his people from their sins." (Matt. 1:21)

From a very early stage in life, we recognize the need to be saved. It starts out simply: as a child, we need saved from a big scary dog or a loud thunderstorm. As we get older, the fears get bigger, the need for saving more intense.

Often, the plethora of fears or circumstances we need saving from can be met with help from our parents, or our friends, or our logic. But there is one circumstance for which we always find ourselves in need of divine intervention, a saving that is out of human hands, and that is salvation from our sin. The choices we make are damaging to others and damaging to our communion with God. From these things, we cannot save ourselves. This is not a recent problem; the pioneer people of God faced this dilemma. But God continues to show up and provide salvation for people like me and you.

Through Jesus, God provided the ultimate salvation. In Jesus, we have someone who can take our sin and right our relationship with God. Considering the enormous sacrifice is awe-inspiring, and that is what has been given to us. As a well-known hymn declares, our sin, "not in part but the whole, is nailed to the cross and I bear it no more. Praise the Lord, praise the Lord, O my soul!"*

—SHANNON L. NEW SPANGLER

TODAY

Ask God to show you the love of Christ our Savior.

---

*Horatio Spafford, "It Is Well with My Soul" (1876).

IMMANUEL

"The virgin will conceive and give birth to a son, and they will call him Immanuel" (which means "God with us"). (Matt. 1:23)

At any given moment in the Christian faith, you may come to a place where you question God. Is God there? Am I just talking to the ceiling? Our faith has highs and lows. At times we struggle to believe that God knows what we are going through, and that God longs to be present with us in it. But when Jesus was born, God became present with humanity on earth. The Divine took on flesh to dwell among us.

This is the major difference between Christianity and every other religion: we affirm that we have a God who took on human flesh and became one of us. Immanuel means "God with us," and in this we can have this confidence: we do not serve a God who is "up there" or "out there" somewhere. We do not serve a God who is distant or hands-off. We serve a God who chose to be one of us, to be present with humanity—a God who is near. When God came in human flesh, he took on human form and feeling. Jesus felt pain and sorrow, happiness and love, the range of human emotions we feel as well.

Come to God confident in the knowledge that our God knows what it is like to be human and chose to be present with us in our humanity.

—SHANNON L. NEW SPANGLER

TODAY

Imagine God is sitting with you now. What do you say?

_____

_____

_____

_____

_____

_____

_____

_____

_____

_____

_____

COMFORTER

He heals the brokenhearted and binds up their wounds. (Ps. 147:3)

During the initial COVID-19 outbreak, I was working as a hospital chaplain. Because of visitation restrictions, there were many times I sat with people who were alone. They were alone as they received bad or hard news, they were alone as they got medical care, they were alone as they processed illness or death. It was truly painful to watch.

Being alone when you are coping with a major life stressor can easily move you into despair. Human beings are created for community and relationship. We need one another, whether it is to help each other process events or just to be present. But the simple truth is there are times when each of us must encounter challenges without immediate support. We have situations we must walk through by ourselves; no one can endure it for us. It is during these times that the role of the Holy Spirit as comforter is especially reassuring.

Scripture reminds us of the comforting presence of the Holy Spirit, who journeys beside me and you through life's most difficult seasons. In circumstances in which we cannot rely on human beings for this comfort, how deeply comforting do we discover our loving God to be? You are promised that God's Spirit is with you always. Are you ready to rely on the Holy Spirit to comfort and heal you in times of desperation and isolation? You do not have to face life alone; the Holy Spirit is present with you.

—SHANNON L. NEW SPANGLER

TODAY

Ask God to show you any part of your heart that needs to be comforted.

COUNSELOR

But the Advocate, the Holy Spirit, . . . will teach you all things and
will remind you of everything I have said to you. (John 14:26)

Have you ever faced a tough decision and wished for someone just to step in and make the decision for you? There are times it might feel like a relief to have someone tell you what to do; that way, you would never be the one responsible for mistakes or choosing the wrong path. As you contemplate major life decisions, consider a new job, or weigh the best way forward in a tough situation, wouldn't it be nice to have a counselor give you advice—someone with wisdom and insight far beyond your own?

When Jesus left Earth, he told the disciples he would send a helper to be with them. This helper would be a counselor to teach them and show them the way. The Holy Spirit is this great counselor for me and you. If we can practice listening for that still, small voice of God, the Counselor will speak to us and teach us in the ways we should go.

Each of us may hear the Counselor through different ways. Some of us sense the Holy Spirit through prayer, others through the wisdom of faithful believers, and yet others through journaling or contemplation. The specific way you connect to the Spirit is not important. Are you taking the time to listen this week?

—SHANNON L. NEW SPANGLER

TODAY

Be silent, make space, and watch for the Spirit leading you.

GOD'S IMAGE GIVEN TO HUMANITY

So God created humankind in his image, in the image of God he
created them; male and female he created them. (Gen. 1:27 NRSV)

While we see God take on many roles in scripture, perhaps the most surprising portrait of God is when he makes humans in his very own image—female and male. Not only do we have a powerful creator God who provides for us, who has saved us and redeemed us, who comforts us in our times of need and teaches us the ways to go, but we also have a God who imparted the image of the very heart of the Trinity into each one of us.

This astounding truth helps us see the intrinsic worth of every single human being—you, me, everyone we encounter, and those we never meet. God has offered humanity a share in God's own life. God has entrusted humanity to be image bearers and to show that image to all the people in our sphere of life. You are called to love like God, to be holy as God is holy, to live with truth and justice and mercy. What a tremendous blessing, what a tremendous calling!

 PRAYER

Almighty God, thank you for revealing yourself to us through scripture,
so that we can catch a glimpse of the ways that you work in
our lives. Encourage us to live the same ways. Amen.

REV. SHANNON L. NEW SPANGLER

resides in Yorktown, Indiana, USA, with her husband and two sons. Ordained in
the Church of God, she is a hospital chaplain and treasurer of the Wesleyan
Holiness Women Clergy board. Shannon has also worked as a senior pastor
and in other ministerial roles. Once, she spent a month traveling
in Israel and participating in an archaeological dig.

DECIDE TO BE WITH GOD

Very early in the morning, while it was still dark, Jesus got up, left the house
and went off to a solitary place, where he prayed. (Mark 1:35)

Have you considered the possibility that what God tells us in prayer is more important than what we can say to God? Jesus knew this and developed an intentional, remarkable, and extremely important lifestyle of prayer: he always reserved moments and space to be with God. Whether morning, afternoon, or night, after being with people, healing the sick, casting out demons, and preaching the good news, Jesus was really busy, giving everything! But praying—being with God and listening to God—was vital.

How do you feel, knowing God anticipates being with you every day, and always wants your company? The heart of God longs for it. There will always be things to do in ministry, daily life, our relationships, making difficult decisions. But like Jesus, you must be vigilant in the very basic things that come first over everything else. The times we live in require that you and I anchor our faith, putting down deep roots in prayer—the line of access to communion with God. God is always ready for you, eager to renew your strength. The Holy Spirit longs for you to receive his encouragement, enjoy his company, and delight yourself greatly. God is faithful to equip us with his grace and wisdom, whatever the challenge.

May prayer be your very lifestyle—deep and real with God! Decide to deliberately seek out God; the results of that decision will be extraordinary. Like Christ, you will know God and his perfect will for your life.

—GRACIELA RAMÍREZ GÁMEZ

TODAY

Choose a space to pray and be with God every day.

TRUST IN GOD

Let us then approach God's throne of grace with confidence, so that we may receive mercy and find grace to help us in our time of need. (Heb. 4:16)

When we are afraid or feel insecure, sad, tired, overwhelmed, or desperate, we look for that special place where we can take refuge, for those people who give us their support, ready to listen to their encouraging words that will alleviate our anxiety. But we do not always find them available. Sometimes we don't get what we think we need.

In what place or person do you prefer to take refuge when you need it most? No matter where you are or how you feel right now, the place and person you really need, you will find available at all times: it is in prayer, with God. Being there is so special; you experience God's presence. God embraces you, offers you his inexhaustible love, and you are renewed. All fear dissipates and your mind is cleared in times of confusion.

God inspired these words to teach us the level of trust we can have in him. We can trust in ways that surpass what we can imagine: God's presence, wisdom, and all his power are for us. God longs to defend us, take care of us, provide for us, and walk by our side in every moment. Be sure to steady your life in prayer. Get fully close to Jesus, your faithful friend! Trust completely in God.

—GRACIELA RAMÍREZ GÁMEZ

TODAY

Write down your fears, experience security, and rest in Christ.

LOOK FOR GOD

You will seek me and find me when you seek me with all your heart. (Jer. 29:13)

The context that the Israelite people lived in was very sad and difficult. They were invaded, expatriated, enslaved, their faith mocked, their liturgical celebrations taken, even to the point of making them deny and forget God. All this suffering was the consequence of not listening to God, not seeking God, and eventually abandoning God. Their spiritual adultery, their idolatry, separated them from the Lord.

In this context, God sent this word of hope to his people, an encouragement to the remnant who remained faithful to him and who suffered because of what others did wrong. God had the perfect timing to remind them he is still God, true to his promises.

Are there circumstances or consequences you are going through today because of those who have sinned, committed injustice, or abandoned God? This is a good time for you to remember who God is: his greatness, power, and faithfulness. It is God who helps you and will continue to sustain you. God has not forgotten you. Though others may have abandoned God, he looks at us and, out of love for us, he will fulfill all his promises.

Have you seen the faithfulness of God in this time? After the catastrophe comes restoration and consolation, among the most beautiful pictures in the entire Old Testament. Seek God with all your heart, no matter what is coming in this life! Keep his Word, seek him wholeheartedly, and you will surely find him.

—GRACIELA RAMÍREZ GÁMEZ

 TODAY

Develop a schedule to intentionally seek God.

DO THE WiLL OF GOD

He fell with his face to the ground and prayed,
". . . not as I will, but as you will." (Matt. 26:39)

What a powerful revelation! Jesus the Son of God, our Savior and Lord, made his lifestyle of prayer visible, sealed with the right attitude and motivations, backed by his obedience and actions.

The crucifixion was a climactic point in the fulfillment of Jesus' mission. Jesus acted in keeping with all he shared from the heart of the Father, and with what he kept in his heart and knew was the will of God through the Holy Spirit. But above all, Jesus acted out of God's love.

In Gethsemane, Jesus was sad, dejected, afflicted: he knew he could open his heart and express himself and ask for what he wanted, so he wouldn't have to endure suffering. Jesus had such security and confidence because he knew the heart of the Father; and yet, Jesus always truly wanted God's will. That is why Jesus decided not to follow his own will or way, but instead chose to do the will of God.

Here, it is worth reflecting that it is not only in doing God's will, but in how we do it, that will reveal our deepest motivations. Surrender your self-will, and choose to do the will of God our Father! Humility and obedience purify our motivations to carry out God's will.

—GRACiELA RAMÍREZ GÁMEZ

TODAY

Write out reasons to trust God's will rather than justifying your own.

KNOW GOD IN THE DESERT

You, God, are my God, earnestly I seek you; I thirst for you, my whole being longs
for you, in a dry and parched land where there is no water. (Ps. 63:1)

There are different types of deserts in the world: complicated, inhospitable
places with extreme geographical conditions. It is said they occupy about a fifth of
the earth's land surface, whether sandy, rocky, arid, polar, or steppe. In scripture,
the most important desert regions include places like the Sinai; the wilderness of
Judea; and the Arabian desert to the east, which separates Judah from Babylon.

We read in scripture of great events that took place in the context of deserts.
For example, the Israelites wandered for forty years in Sinai, where God revealed
himself and accompanied his people with fire by night and cloud by day. God
provided water spouting from the rock and food every day. In scripture, a prophet
fled to the desert to save his life, but it was in the desert that he experienced and
recognized the greatest need of his life, which was God.

The absence of resources in the desert brings to light what is in the heart. In
this context, we discover our actual level of commitment to God—there in the
dryness and adversity in the middle of nowhere. In these difficult times of great
brokenness, God deals with our character. Cling to God and let him expose the
state of your heart. Do not depend on anything else, only him.

—GRACIELA RAMÍREZ GÁMEZ

TODAY

Write memories of your own deserts and the
faithfulness and purposes of God.

LOVE GOD WiTH ALL

Love the LORD your God with all your heart and with all
your soul and with all your strength. (Deut. 6:5)

In Deuteronomy 6:5, the words God gave Moses were strategically and powerfully inspired, with the purpose that God's people, Israel, would know (and have no excuse for not knowing) who God is. This was a command to be rooted and implanted in the minds and hearts of his people and reflected in their actions.

This is how we show the world true relationship with God. We show it with a life that believes in God and depends on him, with this commandment rooted and implanted in the mind and heart, reflected in our actions. The saddest thing about the people of Israel is that they decided not to do that.

In the New Testament, our beloved Jesus takes up this commandment, the biggest and greatest God gives (see Matt. 22:37). To love the Lord our God with all our heart and soul and mind is our biggest and greatest need. It reflects our life in Christ, our reason for living day by day; it is why and who we are and how we serve God in his kingdom. Our thoughts are renewed, our soul quenched by filling that void in the heart.

Then we have the freedom to love God, serving freely and willingly with all our hearts in such a way that people can see God through our very lives. Loving God is our greatest commandment! A fire burns in our hearts and yearns to seek God and love him with all our being.

—GRACIELA RAMÍREZ GÁMEZ

TODAY

Write specific actions you can take to show love and obedience to God.

BE CLEAR MiNDED

The end of all things is near. Therefore be alert and of
sober mind so that you may pray. (1 Pet. 4:7)

Beloved sisters, Jesus Christ our Lord is loving and faithful. He has been pleased to choose us and call us to be with him as his special treasure. It is out of love for Christ that we serve him, seeking him with all our hearts, surrendering self-will in trust. We decided to be Jesus' disciples, willing to trust him, following in his footsteps, honoring his name.

In every crisis or difficulty, even in the desert, there we find him. It is in that place where we know Jesus more intimately; then, we love Christ, remaining faithful by obeying his commandments with firmness and purpose of heart. God helps us have the courage to recognize our strengths and shortcomings, having the confidence that God perfects and enables us every day to please him and be conformed to the image of his Son, Jesus Christ.

Prayer, then, is more than words; it is the most powerful bond that unites us with our God. It is an intentional, permanent lifestyle. How wonderful it is to be with Jesus! It always keeps us clear minded.

PRAYER

God, thank you for loving me! Mold my life to your will, be my true refuge,
and inspire me with the courage to follow you and love you
every day of my life. In Christ Jesus, Amen.

PASTORA GRACIELA RAMÍREZ GÁMEZ

resides in Puebla, México. She is the Wesleyan district superintendent of distrito Sur Iglesia Evangélica Los Peregrinos in México. She served as senior pastor at Iglesia Vida Abundante in Cuautlancingo for twelve years and has courageously served in ministry for thirty-six years. She is married to Pastor Martín Torres. They have two daughters: Graciela, a nutritionist, and Laura, a psychologist.

ARE YOU AWAKE?

The LORD came and stood there, calling as at the other times, "Samuel! Samuel!"
Then Samuel said, "Speak, for your servant is listening." (1 Sam. 3:10)

Early one Sunday morning, a voice suddenly woke me out of a deep sleep. "Are you awake?"

I sat straight up in bed and looked around. My husband was sound asleep. No one else was in the house. I thought I must have been dreaming and promptly lay back down. Not two minutes later, the voice came again.

"Are you awake?"

This was followed by my husband rolling over and smacking my arm, as he continued to sleep. Now I was wide awake! Was I dreaming? Was God speaking? Was someone in the house?

As I prayed about this throughout the day, I searched in scripture about discerning the voice of God. For us to discern the voice of God, we must be in a place to listen.

God revealed a few things to me that Sunday morning, just as he had for Samuel. God knew I needed to be in a place where I could hear his voice clearly. God knew that for me to hear, I needed to be awake and ready for the next chapter he was preparing for me. So often, the busyness of life and circumstances get in the way of being awake, ready to hear the voice of God.

Are you in a situation today in which you are trying to discern the voice of God for the future? Let me encourage you: find a place of refuge to hear from the Lord!

—GINA COLBURN

TODAY

Wake up! Are you listening? Ask God to speak.

WHAT DO YOU WANT FROM ME?

For you were once darkness, but now you are light in the Lord.
Live as children of light . . . and find out what pleases the Lord. (Eph. 5:8, 10)

"Lord! What do you want from me?"

I was the latest budget cut, laid off from a ministry position I had held for six years. As I cried out to God, I desperately wanted to know what would please Christ during this season of my life. At this point, I had been in local church ministry for fifteen years. I wrestled with the question, "Is there more for me?"

For long months leading up to this moment, I had found myself questioning my calling and my role. Being downsized seemed like the perfect opportunity to step out, explore, and move on.

In this moment of crying out, lying prostrate on the floor, seeking honest conversation with God, he clearly spoke to my heart: "Stay as a volunteer."

Growing as children of God, we learn he operates in completely different ways than the world operates. Within a month, I was appointed as interim lead pastor of that congregation, walking the church through one of the most challenging years it had ever faced. Before that unfolded, though, living as God's child meant walking a path that did not make sense at the time.

If it is God who asks you to stay, are you committed to staying—even if it doesn't make sense—so you can walk boldly in the next thing he has for you? God does not make mistakes on the calling he has placed on your life.

—GINA COLBURN

TODAY

If God says stay, stay! Don't let darkness overcome your God-given light.

WHAT'S FOR LUNCH?

But solid food is for the mature, who by constant use have trained
themselves to distinguish good from evil. (Heb. 5:14)

"Mom, I'm hungry!" I heard this phrase multiple times a day when my children were little. When I was a mother to four children ages four and younger, someone was always hungry. It did not take long for me to realize that if I didn't teach my children to feed themselves, I would have a lifelong calling of always being the one preparing meals.

I found this to be true when I became a pastor as well. There were hundreds of people who were hungry for something, but they were not always sure what it was. As a leader, I had to discern how to lead people to the Source of all nourishment, while also feeding myself.

Sometimes, it's easy for women in leadership to take on that kind of "mom" role. At home or in leadership, there is danger if you set aside your own needs to meet the needs of others. To lead well, make sure you are going to the right source for your own nourishment. It's tempting to spend so much time "preparing the meal" for others that you end up forgetting to feed on Christ. Satan would like nothing more than to keep you busy preparing food, so that you miss the feast.

Are you spending your soul time scrolling the latest social media updates, or are you feasting on manna from Jesus? What's for lunch, Jesus? I'm hungry!

—GINA COLBURN

TODAY

Have a meal with Jesus. Ask him to meet your needs.

WHAT'S IN A NUMBER?

Whoever speaks on their own does so to gain personal glory, but he who
seeks the glory of the one who sent him is a man of truth. (John 7:18)

Leading a church from sixty people to four hundred people in six years was no
small task. Many times in the middle of amazing "God moments," deep pain was
going on behind the scenes. It would have been easy to fall prey to the way the
world thinks. Often, I was tempted to buy into the press of success and forget who
really was leading this movement of God.

It is so easy for us to start measuring ourselves by numbers: numbers on the
scale, numbers in the bank account, numbers in our church or small group. Have
you ever begun to see your value based on numbers?

God calls us to something different than that. When you allow God to transform
and renew your mind, you will find you can walk freely in his perfect will without
fear of who might have enviable numbers. You will be able to celebrate all of God's
kingdom wins, because you grasp your own role and calling.

You are not defined by numbers. You are transformed by God. God celebrates
with you when you allow the Holy Spirit to transform and renew you.

Celebrate God's work in you today, no matter how big or small. Buy some
balloons, eat some cake, and worship him for where he has placed you in this
season! You matter!

—GINA COLBURN

TODAY

Throw a party and celebrate the goodness of God.

PURSUING PEACE

If it is possible, as far as it depends on you, live at peace
with everyone. (Rom. 12:18)

"Happy birthday!" Everyone in the room shouted, clapped, and celebrated as the guest of honor unknowingly entered a surprise party. The room was full of joy, laughter, and storytelling. In that happy moment, I felt deep satisfaction; I found it so rewarding to live life with these people and share these milestones.

However, it did not take long for me to begin to feel a little uncomfortable in my spirit. God was prompting my attention toward one of the other guests. Suddenly, my sense of joy was replaced with inner tension. I didn't want to dim a happy occasion, so I ignored the Spirit. But God's words kept echoing persistently in my heart: live at peace!

Honestly, I didn't know there was any disharmony between the two of us, but wanting to be obedient, finally I simply went up to the person and said, "Are we okay?" It was clear at that moment that we were not.

Through that experience, I learned that sometimes living at peace with everyone means listening to the Spirit, doing your part, and leaving the rest to God. When we lead, we will not make everyone happy; not even Jesus did that! But you can live a humble life that experiences the peace of Christ. And it is impossible to experience peace without humility.

—GINA COLBURN

TODAY

Celebrate peace by submitting to the Holy Spirit.

BOLDLY OWNING YOUR CALL

Let us then approach God's throne of grace with confidence, so that we may receive mercy and find grace to help us in our time of need. (Heb. 4:16)

Have you ever felt like "a square peg in a round hole"? Being a woman in ministry often feels like this to me. It can feel like I am always explaining that, yes, I am a pastor. No, I am not the administrative assistant. Yes, women can lead, too. Sometimes I have left events feeling small and without a lot of confidence in who God created me to be. Maybe you can relate.

It's exhausting to push the square peg into the round hole continually. You know this if you have ever watched an infant try to fit shaped blocks to matching holes. Frustration takes over before too long, and defeat is obvious.

I want more for us than exhaustion, frustration, and defeat—and so does God. This text from Hebrews highlights confidence, mercy, and grace. It calls us to boldness. One step I learned to take in living with boldness was to own my calling. When you own your calling, it changes how you enter the room as a "square peg." If you are not invited to the table you want, start your own table. Spending time in God's presence will guide you to discern which table you are called to join.

What table have you been longing to be invited to—or to establish? God wants you to approach the table with confidence and boldness. Have a seat!

—GINA COLBURN

TODAY

Determine where you're trying to fit. Ask God to reveal your table.

TRADING DISTRACTION FOR MASTERPIECE

For we are God's handiwork, created in Christ Jesus to do good works,
which God prepared in advance for us to do. (Eph. 2:10)

In over twenty years of ministry, I spent a lot of time trying to prove I could do whatever my male counterparts did—not only do it but "crush it." Eventually, I became exhausted trying to prove myself in case "they" didn't see my value.

How wonderful to know you are God's masterpiece! God created us to do the work he prepared in advance. How exciting! Let's face it, we might not feel like God's masterpiece every day. We make mistakes, lose our temper with loved ones, or send an email we shouldn't have sent. *There never seems to be enough time to do all the things we think we should be doing.*

God didn't create us to do it all! The Holy Spirit gifted you for a purpose, and it is good and holy. You don't have to walk in someone else's calling to have value. You only need to find your calling and walk in it faithfully. Your talents, gifts, and time are valuable to Jesus and his kingdom.

Your calling may look different with changing seasons, but your value never changes. Discern what drains and detours you; allow God to steer you away from those distractions. You are his masterpiece!

PRAYER

Lord, help us, your daughters, to discern our value and calling from
you and you alone. Ignite in us a passion that draws everyone with
whom we come in contact. We trust you in all things! Amen.

REV. GINA COLBURN

currently resides in Kansas, USA, where she is senior pastor of BreakPointe
Community Church. She has been in ministry for twenty-three years as
a children's pastor, connections pastor, and lead pastor in Pennsylvania
and Kansas for the Northeast District of The Wesleyan Church and the
Church of God (Holiness). Gina has five children and one grandchild.
She and her husband, Jason, founded Forever Yours Ministries.

WORTHY OF WORSHIP

Worship the Lord your God and serve him only. (Luke 4:8)

It was the summer of 1987, and I was a teenage girl living in the pop culture of "a material world." The hair was big, the clothes were bright neon, and the music was Euro-pop dance.

I will never forget the first live concert I attended when I was fifteen years old. It was Duran Duran. My excitement to worship God on Sunday mornings and at youth group paled in comparison to how much I screamed and danced, singing "Hungry Like a Wolf." Without even realizing it, I was worshiping this British pop band. Christian or not, anybody could have taken one look at me and seen clearly that I was a devoted fan, follower, and worshiper—of Duran Duran.

Today, I don't worship a pop band. I know that only God is worthy of worship. And because we were made to worship, there are billions of people on this planet who worship something or someone. Maybe it's not a band; maybe it's a sports team or celebrity or someone closer to home who has become worthy of your attention and devotion. When people look at us, can they tell we are devoted fans, followers, and worshipers of God? Only God is truly worthy of our worship; we were made to worship him only.

—SOO JI ALVAREZ

TODAY

Ask God to identify anything that has a tight hold on your heart.

BACKSTAGE PASS

Since we have confidence to enter the Most Holy Place by the blood of Jesus . . .
let us draw near to God with a sincere heart. (Heb. 10:19, 22)

I was so desperate to meet Duran Duran in person, I listened to the radio every day to see if I could win a backstage pass. At the end of the week, other callers had won passes, but I was not that fortunate.

Today as a more mature Christian, I am reminded that God gives us the ultimate backstage pass. We have direct access to come and meet personally with our holy and loving God.

Have you experienced that place of intimacy? It's a space where all you can do is be in awe of who God is and fall in worship before him. The great, holy God of the universe delights in your praise and has given you "VIP" access into his very presence. When I think about that, I get excited! I have direct access to the most important Being in the universe! I want to shout and yell and sing and dance like I did for Duran Duran.

You can have the confidence of someone with a backstage pass to enter the Most Holy Place and come face-to-face with your loving heavenly Father. God has made a way for you to enter in by the blood of Jesus Christ. So come in and worship just as you are.

—SOO Ji ALVAREZ

TODAY

Worship God knowing that he has given you free access to his presence.

TEARING DOWN VEILS

The curtain of the temple was torn in two from top to bottom. (Mark 15:38)

During the COVID-19 pandemic closures, at some point most people were required to wear face coverings in order to be around others more safely. Many of us are now used to having our faces hidden from each other behind these "veils."

In Scripture, the curtain in the Most Holy Place, which separated God's presence from his people, was torn in two from top to bottom when Jesus breathed his last breath on the cross. The ultimate veil separating us, the beloved bride of Christ, from God has been torn and is no longer there. There is no need to veil yourself or separate yourself from God. There is no need to hide from God, because God has torn down every barrier and separation between him and us.

So stop trying to put the curtain back up between you and God! God has once and for all removed everything we try to hide behind. If you are still experiencing a barrier to God's presence when you worship, ask God to show you what that barrier is. Then ask the Holy Spirit to help you tear it down. Turn from hiddenness and turn back to God who loves you. Boldly enter the holy presence of God, knowing that he has forgiven you and will restore you to your place of transparent worship and intimacy with Christ.

—SOO JI ALVAREZ

TODAY

Ask God to show you why you feel separated in worship.

TRUE WORSHIPERS

Yet a time is coming and has now come when the true worshipers
will worship the Father in the Spirit and in truth, for they are
the kind of worshipers the Father seeks. (John 4:23)

What is a true worshiper? How can you tell if someone is a true worshiper? How can you know if you are a true worshiper?

In this passage, the word *worshiper* is used twice in just one sentence. The truth is that God does not seek our praise. God seeks our hearts. God loves the very presence of the person worshiping, not only the act of worship itself. Christ doesn't require the music we create or the ways we worship through the week with our acts of service. These are only part of how we answer Christ's call to give our whole being, our heart, soul, mind, and strength.

Even though the command to worship the Lord our God has been given to us in the Bible, God does not seek out worship that comes from a sense of obligation or duty. That's not how God created us—to be like robots that worship at the push of a button. God wants true worshipers who worship from love, from the desire for God's presence. God is looking, searching among his Church, to find people who will worship him in the Spirit and in truth. True worshipers give glory to God when it's hard, when it requires sacrifice, when it doesn't feel good, and when the circumstances don't look good. True worshipers know that worship isn't about us; it's about who God is.

—SOO JI ALVAREZ

TODAY

Remember God values you, not just your church participation.

WORSHIP IN THE SPIRIT

God is spirit, and his worshipers must worship in the Spirit and in truth. (John 4:24)

Worship is not about how good we are. Worship is about how good God is. There is a clear drift in Christian culture, and the Church in North America is in danger of worshiping itself. We are in danger of worshiping good music rather than worshiping the One we sing about. We are in danger of worshiping our beautifully built spaces rather than worshiping the Creator who created all things. We are in danger of worshiping our own theology instead of worshiping the One in whom we believe.

When we worship "in the flesh," we begin to worship things constructed by human ambition that can become our false idols. But when we worship in the Spirit, we engage in the spiritual realm and begin to fight the enemy with our songs of victory.

Worship and warfare go hand in hand. In scripture, whenever the people of God failed to worship him with their whole hearts, the enemy defeated them. But when the people of God began to use worship as a tool to fight the enemy, God always gave them the victory. Just as King Jehoshaphat appointed his people to praise God with loud voices at the front of the battlefield (see 2 Chron. 20), you have been appointed by God not only to praise him but to use that praise to fight the enemy. Begin to worship in the Spirit today. As you praise God, you will find that he will fight on your behalf and give you the victory.

—SOO JI ALVAREZ

TODAY

Worship in the Spirit and praise God for the victory.

WORSHIP IN TRUTH

Put off your old self . . . and . . . put on the new self, created to be
like God in true righteousness and holiness. (Eph. 4:22, 24)

God tore down the only barrier left to enter into his presence. But because of fear, pride, sin, or busyness, it's easy to continue to live like there is a barrier between us and God. Do you continue to live like your old self? Do you fear what others will think if you worship with your true self, if you sing loud and off-key, if you cry in despair or shout in anger? Are you ever afraid to admit that you need God?

God wants us to be real with him—to be real with our emotions, real with ourselves. Like anyone else, Christians don't have it all together and we shouldn't pretend that we do. We don't have to sing every song with a smile. God doesn't want you to hide your true self from him and from others; remember Jesus' prayer in Gethsemane? If you desire to experience God's presence in a real way, then be real with God today; worship in truth. God desires your whole self—the real you, and God wants you to be real with him.

Some of us think we've been waiting on God for a long time but have no idea how long God has been waiting on us to be real and truthful. So worship today in the Spirit and in truth, and see what the Holy Spirit will do when you admit you need a Savior.

—SOO Ji ALVAREZ

TODAY

Be real with God and God will be real with you.

FANDOM

You will seek me and find me when you seek me with all your heart. (Jer. 29:13)

One globally popular music group right now is BTS, a Korean "boy band" that took the world by storm. When they gave a free concert in Central Park in New York City, fans waited in line for days; some mega-fans waited for up to five days! One of them, a college student who had seen the band eighty times since 2013, commented, "If you really want something, nothing gets in the way of you having it."

Have you ever wanted something so badly, you'd do anything to get it? Or been so in love with something or someone that you'd do anything to get it or to be with a person? One way to describe this focused action is with the word "seeking." This determined desire to "seek" appears all throughout the Bible. In a world where people are determined to seek out things besides God, we are called to seek him with our whole hearts, to truly be God's biggest fans.

 PRAYER

God, help us seek you in our lives and through our worship. Help us pursue you like heat-seeking missiles until we find you. Help us remember that if we really want you, nothing can get in the way of finding you. Amen.

REV. SOO JI ALVAREZ

is an ordained pastor in the Free Methodist Church. She has been active in ministry for twenty-five years and has been lead pastor at California Avenue Christian Fellowship in Riverside, California, since 2016. She is also board secretary for Wesleyan Holiness Women Clergy. Rev. Alvarez is Korean-Canadian; she and her husband, who is Mexican-American, have a daughter and a son.

THE SPIRIT WHO HOLDS OUR LOSSES

And I will ask the Father, and he will give you another advocate to help you
and be with you forever—the Spirit of truth. (John 14:16–17)

When I was a teenager, my family moved across the country from a small southern town to the Pacific Northwest. This move turned out to be a crucial, life-changing event. Even though it was an experience of my younger years, it proved to be a key part of what I call "God's patterns in my formation."

I was particularly close to one of my younger cousins. We loved spending time together during family visits. Right before we moved, I gave my cousin one of my twin teddy bears. It was symbolic: leaving part of myself behind and finding a way to bring her along with me.

In this text from the Gospel of John, Jesus prepared his disciples for his death and promised them the Holy Spirit—a promise that extends to us today. The Holy Spirit is given to "be with" believers "forever," in times of joy and times of pain. When you find yourself facing the loss of a relationship, a role you loved, or a dream you had, it's very easy to focus and fixate on what is being lost rather than accepting the pain and consequences of the loss. The Holy Spirit has journeyed with me in my patterns of loss. That early experience of moving began to teach me to engage and accept the pain of losses large and small. It also opened the door for me to practice resting in the Holy Spirit's comfort.

—ROMANITA HAIRSTON

TODAY

Receive the comforting Spirit: your advocate against
the enemy and helper in weakness.

MARKED WITH GOD'S SEAL

Don't you know that you yourselves are God's temple and that
God's Spirit dwells in your midst? (1 Cor. 3:16)

Over the years, I've had to focus on what I eat due to a wide range of allergies and severe illnesses. This means paying a lot of attention to food labels and varying "seals of approval" that indicate the label can be trusted. The USDA organic seal is one of the high-quality seals that provides assurance of how food was produced and what is inside it. This is one of many seals I rely on every day to guide me about food items that are essential to my health and well-being.

In today's verse, Paul writes of a different and far more important "seal." In Ephesians 4:30, Paul also wrote that we are "sealed for the day of redemption" with the Holy Spirit. This is remarkably good news to all who believe! The Holy Spirit is a permanent resident in us, marking us as part of God's family called for God's purpose. We are heirs with Christ, and we rest in the protection of a sovereign God. The presence of the Holy Spirit also speaks to what is inside us: faith.

The Spirit is given to those who believe. We are loved and we belong to God. This is a powerful truth in times of doubt about your purpose and call. You and I must answer the question Paul asked the Corinthian church in today's verse. Do you know and believe that you bear God's seal? Do you know that you are God's temple and your life is worship?

—ROMANITA HAIRSTON

TODAY

Let your life shine so those seeing it are drawn to the power of Jesus.

THE EFFORT TO BE FRUITFUL

But the fruit of the Spirit is love, joy, peace, forbearance, kindness, goodness, faithfulness, gentleness and self-control. Against such things there is no law. (Gal. 5:22–23)

I've had countless conversations with powerful women of faith who, at key times in ministry, ask a similar question: "How can I become more fruitful?" One of my dearest mentees struggled with why her ministry was not deepening and blossoming. She'd tell me everything she was doing and where she felt she needed to do more. Over time, our conversations led to her enduring question: what was the real fruit of her ministry? Often, our discussion focused on being versus doing.

These conversations continued through a painful season in her life. I was heartbroken to watch her struggle for greater fruitfulness by doing more through her own effort. I found myself wondering how best to come alongside her, then quickly realized I had to do the same thing I hoped she would: I had to make sure I wasn't trying to "rescue" her with my own wisdom. I had to look to God and let the power of the Holy Spirit flow through me. Each time I was with her, I prayed for God's power to work through me, prompt me, and give me wisdom. It was a holy dance!

Things didn't change overnight, but her life took an amazing turn when she began to partner with the Holy Spirit. Paul's words in Philippians 2:13 remind us that "it is God who works in you to will and to act in order to fulfill his good purpose." You are not alone in your work.

—ROMANITA HAIRSTON

TODAY

Ask God to show you where you're trying to produce your own fruit.

BE FULL OF THE SPIRIT

Jesus, full of the Holy Spirit, left the Jordan and was led
by the Spirit into the wilderness. (Luke 4:1)

I came to faith as a young teen. I don't recall the exact words the preacher said, but I remember the light that shook my soul and opened me to the truth of sin and the power of faith in Jesus to free me from it. It was almost a decade later, right before I turned twenty and accepted my call to ministry, when I came to understand that being sealed with the Holy Spirit was the wonderous beginning of a deeper life in Christ.

I never imagined that I could receive more of the Spirit. I read and studied the many descriptions throughout scripture of Jesus, Peter, Barnabas, Stephen, and others being "full of the Spirit." In those moments, we see them accomplishing amazing things. Our faithful relationship with God and living with God purposefully are key to preparing a life the Spirit fills.

After almost three decades of ministry, I can also remember times when I was close to "running on fumes." Those times weren't caused by lack of the Holy Spirit's presence! There is never a "Spirit shortage." We can enter God's presence by paying attention to spiritual practices, following scripture, being mindful of God's continual company, and engaging with our faith community. When you regularly place yourself in the fullness of God's presence, you can be "prepared in season and out of season" as scripture encourages. Like Jesus, you can walk into the wilderness of your life and walk out of it with victory.

—ROMANITA HAIRSTON

TODAY

Look for the Spirit, whether leaving your Jordan or walking in the wilderness.

WALK IN POWER

But you will receive power when the Holy Spirit comes on you;
and you will be my witnesses in Jerusalem, and in all Judea
and Samaria, and to the ends of the earth. (Acts 1:8)

My kids asked me a lot of questions when they were young. You may remember doing the same thing to your parents or having a nephew or goddaughter pepper you with unending "why," "when," and "how" questions. This childhood habit doesn't necessarily disappear in adulthood; it resurfaces in times of crisis and challenge. In our world, we're often told knowledge is power; it's common to associate knowing with having some form of power.

This verse flips that idea on its head. It releases us from thinking power comes from foreseeing what's ahead or understanding and explaining the complexity of the situations we face. It points us to the truth: power is found in the enduring, unshakable presence of the Holy Spirit. The Spirit is present in your peace, pain, joy, confusion, trial, and triumph.

In the times we're living in, we've come through a triple pandemic: health, politics, and racial tensions. During periods of uncertainty, we long to know answers ourselves and to have answers for those who look to us. I recall the occasions when I've looked at my children's faces after seeing something horrible in the news, or times when I had to preach on the heels of tragedy. Yes, there are things I know, things you know. But in recording Jesus' words, Luke reminds us: your power is not in what you know; your power is in Who you know. The Holy Spirit living in you empowers you to witness in countless ways to the goodness of God and the transforming power of faith in Christ, at any time and in all circumstances.

—ROMANITA HAIRSTON

TODAY

Ask God to show you your assumptions about power.

NOT BY MIGHT NOR BY POWER

So he said to me, "This is the word of the LORD to Zerubbabel:
'Not by might nor by power, but by my Spirit,' says the LORD Almighty." (Zech. 4:6)

What's the hardest thing for you to do right now? For me, it's hard to know how to love those who kill my brothers and sisters in the street. Often, it's in the "trenches" of our lives that we find out where our trust lies. There's no shortage of battles in our world: just open your phone to see a social media post characterized as a battle for the soul of a nation. While it's tempting to avoid the fray, it's an understandable but misplaced instinct.

The last thing our world needs is Christians who become invisible while we endure the storm. Certainly, there are times for prayerful silence. But when we do engage, we have to make sure it's the right battleground. How can we make a difference when so many types of "might" and "power" are being used inside the Church as well as outside it? Paul provided insight: "For though we live in the world, we do not wage war as the world does. The weapons we fight with are not the weapons of the world. On the contrary, they have divine power to demolish strongholds" (2 Cor. 10:3–4).

The Holy Spirit delivers us from seeing brothers and sisters as the enemy, opening our eyes to see that the only side we need to choose is the Lord's side. Then, we fight the right enemy with the right tools. When we focus our energy on casting down the principalities and powers using the full armor of God, the Spirit in us redefines the battle.

—ROMANITA HAIRSTON

TODAY

Rely on the Spirit to see peace overtake the battlefields around you.

ONE IN THE SPIRIT

But when the Advocate comes, whom I will send to you from the Father—the Spirit of truth who goes out from the Father—he will testify about me. (John 15:26)

How can we stay compassionate and connected in trying times? John 16:13 tells us the Spirit will "guide [us] into all the truth." Paul wrote, "The Spirit searches all things, even the deep things of God" (1 Cor. 2:10). Our sealing and filling with the Holy Spirit grants us access to the heart of God. The goal is not to become titans of ministry at the expense of our souls. The Spirit opens a great door for us, so we can walk in the way of Jesus. We know that in the Spirit, we find life, liberty, and power. A life lived in alignment with God's truth is our most aromatic and fragrant worship before the Lord. When it's lived in community, we can see Christ's prayer fulfilled—that we are one. We see a river of compassion flowing in Christian community, a source of restoration and refreshing for all who seek God.

PRAYER

Pray like Christ in John 17: Lord, I pray for all who believe. Let us be one as you are one: Father, Son, and Spirit. May those who believe also be in you, God, so the world may believe you sent Jesus. Open our hearts to be Spirit-filled, working for the unity that only comes through life in you. Amen.

REV. ROMANITA HAIRSTON

has spent almost three decades working in ministry as a preacher and public theologian. Rev. Hairston is a director at Microsoft and president and founder of MORE320. She is a member of the Rainier Avenue Church preaching team. She sits on the boards of Urban Alliance, Urban Impact, Impact Latin America, India Partners, and The Seattle School of Theology & Psychology. Romanita has three children and lives in Seattle, Washington, USA.

CALLED
IDENTITY

PLOT TWIST

Therefore, if anyone is in Christ, the new creation has come:
The old has gone, the new is here! (2 Cor. 5:17)

With many great books, readers can identify a moment that drew them in and captured their attention. Page after page, you find yourself visualizing characters, scenes, and sometimes trying to guess where the storyline will go. Then in a way you wouldn't ever expect, the author takes you down an unforeseen path and it blows your mind completely! It's a plot twist, and readers are captivated. When an author draws you into a story, you begin to assume you know where the plot is headed, so you settle in, expecting familiar things. But every plot twist moment takes you out of the same old story line, capturing your imagination for the unexpected places a story can go. It's transformational.

In this letter to the people of Corinth, Paul reminded his audience then and now of the way Christ transformed the plot of our story. When you and I take on the identity of a follower of Christ—plot twist! We become part of the new creation. This new creation story transforms us daily, and it will continue to transform us as we lean into it.

Paul reminded the early Christians that the old story line is gone and the new one is here. Do you need a reminder today of God's plot twists in your life? Remember to abide in the fullness of your identity in the new creation.

—ASHLEY GAGE

TODAY

Prayerfully reflect on God's grace in your story, plot twists and all.

REMEMBER WHO YOU ARE

See what great love the Father has lavished on us, that we should
be called children of God! And that is what we are! (1 John 3:1)

Who are you? Has anyone asked lately? This question can be answered in so many ways, depending on what information is wanted. Is it a name, a lineage, a position, a title? Or does the answer require pause and reflection? There are so many ways to answer this simple question; depending on the scenario in which it is asked, all these responses could be technically accurate yet still incomplete.

As followers of Christ, when we are called to respond to the question, "Who are you?" we have a name, lineage, and title that are beyond compare! In this letter, John powerfully urged his readers and us today to remember this name, lineage, and title. In God's great love for us, he gives us a new name, a new identity, a lineage and a title. We are called children of God!

Not only are we called to remember our identity as God's children, we are also reminded of who we belong to! And in a world where we are constantly asked to identify ourselves by our accomplishments and roles, it is vital to remember whose we are. As children of God, when you and I remember who we are in Christ, we are able to reflect the lavish love of God to a world full of people that don't know who they are—or who God is.

—ASHLEY GAGE

TODAY

Remember who you are in Christ today; reflect on God's lavish love.

MISTAKEN IDENTITY

Am I now trying to win the approval of human beings, or of God?
Or am I trying to please people? (Gal. 1:10)

Chef Megan was a pastry chef trainee learning at a fancy restaurant. Her executive chef tasked her to prepare a special order for a private event. Her job was to make sugar-free chocolate mousse for one hundred people. She completed the tricky dessert very successfully—or so she thought. As she looked across the ingredients she had used, she realized that she had included the wrong sweetening agent. The dessert was not in fact sugar-free. Although the mousse looked and tasted amazing, it had a mistaken identity! Quickly, she whipped up a new batch, ensuring the second batch of mousse could indeed claim the title of sugar-free. (Don't worry, both batches found their way to grateful recipients; no chocolate mousse was sacrificed in this mistake!)

Just like the mistaken sugar in a "sugar-free" dessert, you and I can find ourselves leaning into a false identity when we fall into the trap of wanting or vying for the approval of humans and not God. Those who are called to serve Christ in ministry are not exempt from this trap; in fact, people-pleasing can be one of the biggest causes of a mistaken identity. Paul's pointed questions to the Galatians should remind us to double-check our sense of identity today. As a servant of Christ, are you living for Christ or for the approval of human beings?

—ASHLEY GAGE

TODAY

Pray for the courage to live for Christ above everything else.

OUTFIT OF THE DAY

Therefore, as God's chosen people, holy and dearly loved, clothe yourselves
with compassion, kindness, humility, gentleness and patience. (Col. 3:12)

In our current digital age, there is an intriguing fashion trend. On social media, you can find a popular hashtag for "outfit of the day" or #OOTD. Fashion influencers use it to share daily outfits with their followers. Most of us make a daily choice of what we will wear as well. Sometimes you put on clothes and the fit and look are perfect; other times, clothing seems to magically shrink in the closet, and the fit isn't what you remember. Sometimes an outfit serves a specific purpose, so each item must match that purpose. Perhaps an outfit must have what all women want: pockets!

The #OOTD that children of God are called to wear must also be chosen daily, serving a specific purpose: to reflect the image of God in the world. As God's dearly loved children, we are called to put on the clothing of compassion, kindness, humility, gentleness, and patience. The fashion for children of God should be a perfect fit, right? Perfectly sized every time you put it on. But sometimes these pieces just don't fit right: one day, gentleness is hard to put on, or patience seems to shrink on occasion. So what happens when the outfit doesn't fit quite right?

As we continue to clothe ourselves as God's dearly loved children, through the power of the Holy Spirit at work in and through us, our spiritual clothing will become the perfect fit for every occasion.

—ASHLEY GAGE

TODAY

Review the attributes in this verse; are you wearing them today?

FINDING THE RIGHT ROUTE

Show me your ways, LORD, teach me your paths. Guide me in your
truth and teach me, for you are God my Savior. (Ps. 25:4–5)

In many parts of the world, modern navigation is incredible; with a global positioning system, or GPS, I can input my destination into a smartphone, knowing I will be guided to my stop by the most efficient route. I can even set my GPS to avoid construction, highways, tollways, or anything that might delay my journey. I no longer have to fumble with folding a paper map that doesn't depict the best routes or road closures. But as amazing as GPS technology is, it isn't perfect, sometimes due to the error of the person using it, sometimes due to flaws in the technology itself.

In our walk with God, we need direction and guidance. As those called to minister and share the Gospel, it's vital that we take a route focused on the right destination. Our destination is always to know Christ more fully every day.

This psalm reminds me how to choose the right destination for my life every day. When I surrender the desire to make my own path and allow the Lord to teach and guide me instead, I position myself to know God more fully. By placing your hope in God all day long, you will allow your steps to stay on course. "Operator error" may occur at times, but you can be sure God will never lose sight of you or lead you down the wrong path. So we pray today and every day, "Lord, show me your ways."

—ASHLEY GAGE

TODAY

Pray this verse today in faith.

ALL WE NEED

His divine power has given us everything we need for a godly life through our knowledge of him who called us by his own glory and goodness. (2 Pet. 1:3)

Preparing for a vacation can, ironically, be tiring: ensuring your travel arrangements are secure, packing essential things you will need for the trip, and trying to proactively prepare for any travel interruptions that could unfold. Then, there are arrangements to make for the time you'll be away from normal activities: making sure your workload is covered, your home attended to—the list could go on and on. It might even feel like the process is not worth the actual vacation! But once you are relaxing and enjoying your rest, you realize it was completely worth the hassle.

Sometimes as we grow in our faith, it's tempting to create long, exhaustive lists of things we need to complete in order to move closer to God. Maybe you try to plan your walk with Christ just like you might plan a trip away. But if I try to limit my relationship with Christ to a checklist, I will completely miss out on the goodness of God. In his letter, Peter affirmed that everything we need to live a godly life is not found in our own strength and power, but rather through God's divine power—God, who called us by his own glory and goodness. Today, God invites you to participate in the journey of faith; he provides all you need.

—ASHLEY GAGE

TODAY

Consider whether you try to control how God works in your life.

THE STORY I'LL TELL

And I pray that you, being rooted and established in love, may have power,
together with all the Lord's holy people, to grasp how wide and
long and high and deep is the love of Christ. (Eph. 3:17–18)

There is a rich history passed down from generation to generation, one that will always be around: the art of storytelling. Whether grandparents pass down family memories to grandkids, or locals share origin stories to the next generation, or someone writes a memoir of a life well lived, the telling of these stories changes the hearer. Each story shapes the person receiving the story in a new way.

The same is true of the gospel story: once we step into God's story and take on the identity of a child of God, our whole life is transformed. God loves you so deeply, and it's out of that deep love God shows you that you can love God and others. The story of God's steadfast, transformational love is the story that will never grow old or go out of date. As a child of God, you are invited to participate in God's story, and oh, what a story you have to tell!

PRAYER

Gracious God, thank you for inviting me into your story! Thank you
for loving me with steadfast, never-changing love and calling me your child.
When I am pulled by the world to lose sight of my identity,
remind me of who you say I am. Amen.

PASTOR ASHLEY GAGE

is associate chaplain at Northwest Nazarene University. She previously
served for three years as connections pastor at Nampa College Church in
Idaho, USA. She is an adult transracial adoptee and mother of twins.
Ashley loves spending time with her family and musical theater.

STEPPING IN TO YOUR CALL

The LORD said to Joshua son of Nun, Moses' aide: "Moses my servant is dead. Now then, you and all these people, get ready." (Josh. 1:1–2)

I was in shock the day my youth pastors told me they were moving. While I was a college student, they had been my primary mentors for nearly six years—like spiritual parents. I was an intern, soaking up their wisdom and pastoral character. Their guidance gave me confidence, knowing that if I followed in their footsteps, I too could lead in ministry. But without their presence, could I lead the ministry they had grown?

Moses left a massive legacy, having led the Hebrew people out of slavery and setting up a new way of life with God on their journey to the promised land. Moses' death marked a transition of leadership and direction for a large community. The Lord called Moses' apprentice, Joshua, to lead the nation. Joshua would not just lead through the wilderness but would guide the people of God into the long-awaited promised land.

Mentoring is foundational to knowing and experiencing God's call. When we watch others lead and we learn from them, we find our own sense of how to be and do as we clarify the Lord's direction in our life.

Inevitably, there comes a point of transition, when as an apprentice you must choose to step fully into your own identity and God-given authority to lead. It may feel overwhelming, but just as Joshua knew, your calling does not originate with you but with God. Your faithfulness is demonstrated simply in responding to God's invitation in that moment.

—TRISHA WELSTAD

TODAY

Seek out mentors; acknowledge your call so you can prepare to respond.

STRATEGIC PREPARATION

Get ready to cross the Jordan River into the land
I am about to give to them—to the Israelites. (Josh. 1:2)

Preparing for change is a multilayered experience. It includes dimensions like the mental process to transition from what is, to what is next; the inner emotional reality and cues of your body as you experience the transition; and for many, the physical exertion of preparation: list-making, clearing out, gathering for the new needs ahead. A transition may be relocation, a new educational endeavor, or a new role. But whatever it looks like, conscious and subconscious planning is happening.

God instructed Joshua to lead preparations for change, both for himself and the entire community of the Israelite people. Their time of wandering was at an end; a transition of leadership and location was in full effect. Moving an entire community of people from the place that had become home to the new home they had long anticipated would engage all these dimensions of planning.

Joshua's response to the Lord's instruction was to offer a detailed process for the Israelites to get prepared. He told them to get their supplies ready, offered a timeline of three days, and communicated where they would cross the river and where they would go. He used his leadership to provide concrete action steps to lay out their path forward.

At times, your calling will require strategic preparation. There will be much change ahead for you and for your community. As a leader, take time to lean into God's vision and clarify how that vision informs your preparation. This preparation on your own part will help you create space to be fully present in activating your community to follow God's call.

—*TRISHA WELSTAD*

TODAY

Actively prepare yourself to live into the fullness of your call.

THE GENEROSITY OF GOD

I will give you every place where you set your foot, as I promised Moses. (Josh. 1:3)

Children often feel that they can go anywhere or do anything. Jump out of a tree? Yes! Yell at the top of their lungs? For sure. Eat four slices of cake without getting sick? Absolutely. It's not until they harm themselves or are given boundaries by others that they grasp that there are limits to who they are and what they can do.

But unfortunately, as we grow, we may end up limiting ourselves to a much smaller territory than what God has actually called us to inhabit. We might make agreements with ourselves that cause us to "play small" in order to fulfill others' expectations. We may live from a place of scarcity to prevent judgment from our peers. We may put the calling that was present within us as a young person to the side for a more "practical" life. Have you ever traded invincibility for smallness?

The promise to Moses was reiterated to Joshua. God planned to be just as faithful to the next generation of his people, not limiting them to something smaller than originally planned. They were welcome to take the promised land to settle their families and community.

God's faithfulness to his promises also threads through your life. In the midst of the joy and grief you will inevitably encounter, God's generosity is never limited toward you. God invites you not to shrink to fit others' plans, but to grow into your calling with boldness.

—TRISHA WELSTAD

TODAY

Gently refuse to settle; boldly believe in God's generosity toward you.

SETTING SPACIOUS BOUNDARIES

Your territory will extend from the desert to Lebanon, and from the great river, the Euphrates—all the Hittite country—to the Mediterranean Sea in the west. (Josh. 1:4)

When I think of boundaries, I picture lines drawn on maps that show borders of countries, charting where one territory ends and another begins. I also picture fences between one home and a neighbor's home, marking space to show where someone can dwell and what belongs to them. Interpersonally, boundaries reflect where you end and someone else begins.

In your calling, there are more markers of who you are and who you are not. The more life experience and wisdom you gain, the more you begin to learn, "this is me" or "this is definitely not me." Each time I mentor someone in discerning their calling, I tell them, "This is a 'taste and see' opportunity." In other words, their experiential learning produces vocational discernment, defining the boundaries of who they are—and who they are not.

In this verse, God was giving borders to the Israelites. The boundaries God set for them showed them the exact lines of their territory: what they would possess and what they would not. They would get to explore the spaciousness of the land provided for them. Their identity would be marked by the location they inhabited.

God is good to you in giving you a calling with borders, so that you don't attempt to be everything to everyone, and so that you also realize that you are still someone. The clearer you become in your identity and calling, the easier it is to allow others to be the fullness of who God made them to be.

—TRISHA WELSTAD

TODAY

Explore your calling so you can clarify your identity.

SECURE IN YOUR HOPE

No one will be able to stand against you all the days of your life. (Josh. 1:5)

In American culture, worry is normative. Though we want movies to have happy endings, we also absorb stories of uphill battles "against the odds." Worrying about the unknown future, however, affects how we engage the present.

For others, repeated trauma can give way to wariness and hypervigilance. The uncertainty of what might be floods your body with anxiety, making joy seem distant.

Either way, how might we allow God to gently untangle habitual worry or vigilant anxiety tightening around our calling? After the scarcity of the wilderness, is there still room for you to hope—to live into God's call? When you emerge from bombardment, overcome by rejection, failure, or the judgment of others, is there space to regain security in who you are and how you can live out your call?

After years as people trying to survive the desert, Israel trusted God's offer of security as they followed him. God's people could depend on God, who offered peace, abundance, and secure presence in their new home. While they didn't know their future, they found a way to trust God's words in their transitional circumstance.

You are seen and called by this same God, who still invites humans to trust. Made in God's image, entrusted with a calling, you are invited to trust him with your fragile hope for a freeing future. As you practice trusting God's goodness, you will be free to truly be yourself, free to live into your calling with authenticity. God actively stands with you each day; no one can steal that reality. Your hope isn't wasted; your calling is sure.

—TRISHA WELSTAD

TODAY

Ask God what you need to entrust to him; remember, your calling is sure.

CALLING IS COMMUNAL

As I was with Moses, so I will be with you;
I will never leave you nor forsake you. (Josh. 1:5)

Moving to a different state to start a new ministry felt exciting and like a lonely journey all at once. After living in Southern California for nearly a decade, moving back to the Northwest was hard. I knew I was called to move, but Portland had never been home for me. Friends who had become like family, a culture to which my family had adapted—these were now a thousand miles away. Yet, there was something I knew I was being called to do in Portland.

Sometimes following God's call is overwhelming; you may need reminders that you are not alone.

Throughout scripture, God reminds his people of his presence going with them. For Joshua, God reminded him of the past; just like God had been with Moses, he would also be faithful to Joshua. Beyond God's reminder to Joshua of his presence in the present, God reassured Joshua that he would be able to rely on his presence in the future as well.

Even in times of radical change, your calling is always communal. God is consistently with you and calls you to remember the empowering presence of the Holy Spirit. Remembering that God is with you can reconnect you to the source of your calling when you face overwhelming new circumstances. Reconnecting will remind you that you are partners with God; your actions are not solely dependent on you. As a leader, living as the incarnational presence of God will create community wherever you go—community within you and community around you.

—TRISHA WELSTAD

TODAY

Partner with God in your call; God is already with you!

WALK IN YOUR AUTHORITY

Be strong and courageous, because you will lead these people to inherit
the land I swore to their ancestors to give them. (Josh. 1:6)

"How you do anything is how you do everything," my coach always says. When I am weighing how I am going to show up for my kids or plan for a meeting that feels daunting, I remember these words. When I think about self-care and how I show love for God, myself, and others, these words come to mind.

God's call to Joshua and the people of Israel was to be strong and courageous. Three different times in the first nine verses of Joshua, the Lord said to be strong and full of courage. The people were given instructions; they were not alone, they had nothing to dread, and their calling was from God. The imperative is that they should get their strength from God's presence with them and bravely move into their future. They were to walk in their God-given authority.

When you act trusting God's anointing on your life, you will find yourself able to walk in your God-given leadership authority.

PRAYER

God, I know you want to give me courage to follow you wherever you lead.
I ask for that courage today. Show me that you always walk beside me and that I
lead anointed by the authority of your Spirit for your kingdom and glory. Amen.

REV. DR. TRISHA WELSTAD
is an ordained Free Methodist elder and has ministered in churches in Los Angeles and Oregon. Trisha is the executive director of the Leadership Center and directs the Institute for Pastoral and Congregational Thriving at Portland Seminary. She has a doctoral degree in leadership and global perspectives. Trisha and her family live in Portland, Oregon, USA, where they enjoy exploring the outdoors and throwing parties.

WHAT ARE YOU MODELING?

After that, he poured water into a basin and began to wash his disciples' feet,
drying them with the towel that was wrapped around him. (John 13:5)

My young adult nephew lives with me. After a while, I noticed that if I fold the bath towels in half, he does the same with his towel. If I fold the towels in thirds, so does he. This pattern was repeated: where I placed things in the fridge, the shoes in the hallway, and so on. Then it dawned on me—he was modeling and mirroring my behavior. My next immediate thought was, I better be modeling the right thing, because someone is following me!

Here in the Gospel of John, Jesus washed the disciples' feet, modeling servant leadership. His act of humility reminds me that I must lead with humbleness of spirit. I saw this type of leadership modeled in some excellent mentors.

One was a seminary professor who taught Greek on weekdays and a kindergarten Sunday school class on weekends. When asked why he would "waste his talents" teaching kindergarteners, he replied, "If I can't communicate the gospel to five-year-olds, then I don't really know it!"

In his example, I saw someone willing to serve in capacities others might deem below his level of education and attainment. Kind of like Jesus, stooping to do a job usually reserved for the lowest member of the household. With other examples I've encountered from time to time, his example prompted me to reflect on my own posture toward servanthood. What exactly am I modeling? What story is my life writing? Is it worthy of being repeated?

—KIM GLADDEN

TODAY

Do an act of service this week that models humility.

HOW DO YOU DEAL WiTH ENEMiES?

'He who shared my bread has turned against me.' (John 13:18)

It was a hard, sad day when I realized someone I had mentored, someone I had given opportunities in ministry, had betrayed me. I kept thinking, "After all I've done, how could you treat me like this?" And I've had the "growth opportunity" of this happening more than once—which is why today's scripture confronts me.

Jesus, knowing there was an enemy present, still shared bread and fellowship with him. Judas is at the table with Jesus and the other disciples. Judas got his feet washed by Jesus. Judas gets to leave the room alive to go betray Jesus. In fact, Judas is told, "What you are about to do, do quickly" (John 13:27). And with this example, my idea of how enemies should be treated is stretched.

I'm not to be naïve or gullible, but I am challenged to consider how I deal with enemies. This just might be a measure of my emotional health. What if my capacity to deal well with enemies is also a marker of spiritual maturity?

I've challenged myself in this area. I've intentionally tried to resist the temptation to get even with enemies, instead trying to understand what might compel their actions. When I do this, I often find my anger and hurt deflated. Many times it has turned an enemy into a friend (or at least a "frenemy"). It's not always pleasant, but I'm learning how to treat even my enemies well.

—KiM GLADDEN

TODAY

Examine how you react to those who turn against you.

GROWING ROOM

"Will you really lay down your life for me? Very truly I tell you, before
the rooster crows, you will disown me three times!" (John 13:38)

There are certain muffin recipes I have that give this admonition about placing batter in the baking tin: "Do not overfill—they will expand during baking." The recipe creator is telling me to allow room for growth.

Sometimes I have to keep this in mind in relationships I have. I have to keep reminding myself that people grow at different rates and sometimes need the experiences they are going through to help them grow.

That's what I see Jesus doing with Peter. Jesus knows that Peter will deny him and even gives the timeframe for it happening—before the rooster crows. Jesus also knows it will happen not once but three times. Yet Peter is not banished forever from the presence of Jesus. He is allowed opportunity to make his mistakes and grow, which he does. Then he is invited to restored relationship.

There are people in my life I wish I could spare from life's lessons. And yet, sometimes, their very failures are a part of what makes their journey unique.

As someone who likes to be in control, this is a challenge for me—to allow others room to make mistakes and grow. I keep thinking, if you would just receive wise advice and counsel, you could avoid that pitfall! But look at Peter. He goes on to be a pillar of New Testament Church life. He was one forgiveness away from greatness.

—KIM GLADDEN

TODAY

Offer forgiveness to someone who has wronged you.
It may be the way back to a restored relationship.

THE TROUBLE WITH TROUBLE

"Do not let your hearts be troubled. You believe in God; believe also in me." (John 14:1)

It's hard to do, but it can be done. Jesus tells his disciples not to let their hearts be troubled. I believe Jesus is insinuating that you can walk through trouble without being troubled. It makes me think of a high-wire walker. This kind of activity takes incredible focus, concentration, practice, and skill. It is not easily accomplished by the uninitiated.

But the trouble with trouble is that it's troubling. There was a time in my life when I was in another country, and I was under threat of arrest because I was a Christian. It felt quite harrowing, right up until the night of my supposed arrest. That night, the presence of the Lord overshadowed me, and I could hear God saying, "I'm going to get you out." I had no idea how, but after that I turned over and slept like a baby. And sure enough, miraculously, I was not arrested but allowed to return to the United States. I keep remembering that time as a reference point, a moment of perspective whenever I'm facing trouble. If God could get me out of that situation and assure me with his sustaining presence, I can also be assured and sustained in what I currently face. And what is that perspective? It's echoed here in Jesus' words, "Trust in God, trust also in me."

—KIM GLADDEN

TODAY

Reframe a situation you currently face with a God-focused perspective.

ARE YOU READY TO RECEIVE?

"And I will ask the Father, and he will give you another
advocate to be with you forever." (John 14:16)

One time, I wanted to bless a friend of mine. I picked out gifts with great detail and care as I went to little shops all over Europe, assembling a tower of delightful things I planned to give him upon my return to the United States. I put the gifts in cascading little boxes. Then I tied a blue satin ribbon around all of the boxes and topped the tower with a bow. I was beaming with anticipation of how surprised and delighted he would be when he opened the gifts, each one exceeding the other in value. But the surprise was on me. When I returned, my friend was engaged to another woman and never came to pick up the gifts. All my good intentions came to nothing; he was not in a place to receive.

Here in the Gospel of John, Jesus speaks about a gift he is promising to give. Jesus promises the gift of the Holy Spirit, a forever advocate. Note the care and detail he gives about the gift in the surrounding verses. And yet, as good as his intentions and gift are, it all comes to nothing if we won't receive it. Why have a gift and not open it? I want to live in a posture of openness to the counsel and comfort of the Holy Spirit. Don't you?

—KIM GLADDEN

TODAY

Receive the gift of the Holy Spirit as Counselor.

iS YOUR HEAD iN THE SAND?

"I will not say much more to you, for the prince of
this world is coming. He has no hold over me." (John 14:30)

To be healthy, there are times we must acknowledge painful truths: truths about ourselves, our loved ones, our situation, or more. So while you and I can keep a God-focused perspective on our troubles, we can't live in unreality, pretending they aren't there. Otherwise it sounds like the troubles are living in unreality.

Look at Jesus. After this poignant time of ministry and fellowship at the Last Supper, he begins to set his mind, preparing his disciples for what is ahead, for what is coming next. What is coming? Jesus says the prince of the world is coming. The implication is that it won't be good times and laughs for all.

I love that God gives us the grace to acknowledge painful truths and difficult realities. There was the day I completed a family genogram and was hit with the stark reality that there lay my one little circle with no connecting lines—no husband or children to draw lines to. I was faced with the fact that when I'm gone, that's the end of my line. It took a moment to absorb the shock. I've handled my singleness well and tried to model what it means to live for Christ as an unmarried, mature Christian adult, but I was still unprepared for that moment when it hit home. But hit home it did. I faced it, and then I moved on. When you and I are living in healthy spirituality, we are not afraid to acknowledge even painful truths.

—KiM GLADDEN

TODAY

Examine which truths you need to acknowledge and submit to God.

WHAT MODEL OF CHRISTIANITY DOES YOUR LIFE DISPLAY?

"But [the prince of this world] comes so that the world may learn that I love the Father and do exactly what my Father has commanded me." (John 14:31)

One time I visited a Caribbean island while leading a mission team of college students. On our way to the more remote areas of the island, we spent the first night in the capital city, girls in one room, boys in the other. The next morning the maid came to me and said, "Reverend, I found this in the boys' room." It was a business card for a place where scantily clad women danced. She asked, "Is this a place for Christian men to go?" I assured her it was not, that I didn't think our guys had been there but would check it out. They hadn't been there, but the cab driver on the way to the hotel had given it to one of them, who threw it on the dresser, thinking nothing of it. The point is that the world is watching! So let us live lives of spiritual health and vitality that, like Jesus, model that we do exactly what the Father has commanded us.

PRAYER

Dear Lord, let my life be a healthy and compelling witness to who you are. Meet me with your grace in the areas where I need growth. Release the power of your Holy Spirit in me continually, I pray. Amen.

REV. KIM GLADDEN

is the director of discipleship for The Wesleyan Church. Prior to that role, she led as a pastor, church planter, missionary, and university chaplain. With an MDiv from Colgate Rochester Divinity School and an undergraduate degree in business management from Florida A&M University, Rev. Gladden has been at home in congregational ministry as well as teaching and leading in university settings. She is the founder of the VisionQuest Christian Orchestra and VisionQuest Ministries (a mission service organization).

JOY AND CONFUSION: WHEN GOD IS DOING SOMETHING

The angel went to her and said, "Greetings, you who are highly favored! The Lord is with you." Mary was greatly troubled at his words. (Luke 1:28–29)

Ana was ten years old when her mother and grandmother asked what she wanted to be when she grew up. Very sure of herself, Ana replied: "I'm going to be a pastor." Mom and Grandma burst out laughing. This confused Ana greatly. "Why are they laughing at me? Did I say something wrong? Don't they believe me? Could it be that I cannot be a pastor?"

Even at her young age, Ana had a close relationship with God; she prayed, read the Bible daily, and actively participated in all that her church had to offer. In her experience with God, she was clear that the Lord had called her into ministry; and Ana received and accepted that call with great joy. But the laughter of her family caused her confusion. She didn't know that they weren't laughing at her call but simply at how cute she looked when she answered.

When Mary received the message from the angel announcing the call she could fulfill, there was also a mixture of joy and confusion. On one hand, questions of "how" or "why me" would naturally arise; while on the other hand, the joyous expectation arose that God was about to do something, and she was a part of it.

Throughout your ministry, you will go through some seasons of great joy, others of confusion. Through them all, God will be with you and will affirm your calling.

—MARY ANN MARTÍNEZ

TODAY

Identify things that bring you joy; thank God for each one.

DOUBT AND ANXIETY: I'LL FIX IT

Sarai his wife took her Egyptian slave Hagar and gave her
to her husband to be his wife. (Gen. 16:3)

Years ago, I went with my sister and niece to a beauty salon that was just across a bridge. While there, it started to rain heavily. The owner advised us to leave, because the river was capable of rising until it covered the bridge; this could make it dangerous to cross. Instead, we decided to wait for the rain to pass and continued having our hair done.

By the time we were finished, the angry waters had indeed covered the bridge, and the rescue truck that helped people cross was already gone. While we were at the salon, my older brother crossed to our side with the help of the truck. Now we were on the same side, without help.

The force of the river was sweeping away everything in its path. We waited three hours, but nothing seemed to change. We debated: "Do we wait or risk walking across?" The bridge was not visible; was it still there? By then, I could see my husband across the river, signaling to stay still and wait.

My brother got desperate, took us by the hand, and pulled us across the river, walking on a bridge we could not see. It almost cost us our lives.

God had been clear in his promise to Sarai. She got desperate and risked a lot.

While we wait, it may seem that nothing is changing. But the waters are receding, little by little. Do not cross the bridge too early.

—MARY ANN MARTÍNEZ

TODAY

Stop your rushing; wait for God's moment.

LOSS AND HURT: SPIRITUAL NUMBNESS

When the Lord saw her, his heart went out to her and he said, "Don't cry." (Luke 7:13)

We are integrated beings. Our dimensions are interconnected, interrelated. When you are in pain, your emotions are affected. When you are sad, your body feels tired. Emotionally, we go into shock at unexpected news, into denial when reality is too harsh. Your spiritual life is also affected by the circumstances and experiences you live through.

When Carmen received the news that the mass found in her left breast tested positive for cancer, she went into a state of shock. She understood the words she was hearing, but she couldn't comprehend what they meant for her. To her, the oncologist was talking about someone else. The doctor explained the stage of her cancer, treatment alternatives, recommendations, and the prognosis. Carmen listened, but she couldn't absorb it. As the doctor talked, she simply "checked out." She felt numb.

Days passed; a long journey began. Carmen can remember how slowly the feelings of loss, pain, fear, and anguish arose. But the thing that surprised her the most was the spiritual numbness. During it all, she felt that she could not connect to God.

Still, Jesus was close to Carmen, just as he was to the widow who was mourning her dead son. Her pain and loss didn't lead her to pray or cry out for a miracle. Nevertheless, she received an answer that she didn't even ask for.

God is at work in your life, even when you don't have the strength to cry out to him.

—MARY ANN MARTÍNEZ

TODAY

Write down feelings you are having now; pray over each one.

FEARFUL AND FEARLESS: WiTHOUT STOPPiNG

God is our refuge and strength, an ever-present help in trouble. (Ps. 46:1)

Fear has a bad reputation. People are told not to be afraid, and in many cases, fear is considered a weakness. Often when we are fearful, we think there is something wrong with us. Sometimes, we even define fear as opposed to faith, meaning that where there is faith, there is no fear. Therefore, we conclude, the fearful person has no faith.

However, fear is a part of the human experience. Under certain circumstances, it can help us. Fear is what makes us cautious; it is what makes us protect ourselves in times of danger. Thanks to fear, we can react to circumstances that are not safe. At times like these, fear may be necessary.

At the same time, if we allow fear to engulf our lives, it can paralyze us and prevent us from advancing in what God wants. In those moments, fear can damage us.

The Bible tells us that when we are in God's hands, we are safe. When we are in the hands of the Most High God, we do not need to save ourselves; it is God himself who covers us.

Today, you are in the hands of a God who loves and guards you and those you love. The next time you feel fear, remember that God is your refuge and strength.

—MARY ANN MARTÍNEZ

TODAY

Do something that fear prevented you from doing, trusting God.

BETRAYED AND FAITHFUL: EMBRACING THE MIRACLE

"You are the God who sees me," for she said,
"I have now seen the One who sees me." (Gen. 16:13)

Her name was Lucy, but few knew it. She loved music and art, and she was an excellent writer. Nobody knew. Lucy had no friends. She grew up in a home where her father was always drunk and her mother was too depressed to take care of her. Her older siblings left home as soon as they were self-sufficient; none of them returned for her. Throughout her whole life, she was emotionally neglected.

Lucy always felt invisible and now, in adulthood, there was no difference. Her romantic relationships ended in a cycle of indifference that increasingly undermined her self-worth. No one seemed to notice her at work. As much as she struggled, she could not shake the feeling of not belonging; she always felt like an outsider.

Hagar was invisible in her home. Like Lucy, she was surrounded by people who did not notice her, except when they wanted to use her for the benefit of others. Those whom she served were not able to truly see her; they only noticed what she could give them.

Hagar's story teaches us that invisibility before others does not mean invisibility before God. The Lord not only saw Hagar, but he also worked a miracle in her life and gave her a promise. God's work in our lives does not depend on our living conditions or what others think—or do not think—of us. God always sees you.

—MARY ANN MARTÍNEZ

Forgive those who have made you feel invisible; embrace your miracle.

CHALLENGES AND LEADERSHIP: BIGGER THAN YOURSELF

Now Deborah, a prophet, the wife of Lappidoth,
was leading Israel at that time. (Judg. 4:4)

Born into slavery, Harriet Tubman escaped in 1849. Far from staying safe and enjoying her newfound freedom, Tubman decided to risk everything to lead other enslaved people to freedom. So, based on her own experience of escape and a firm conviction that God was guiding her, she devised plans, mapped out routes, and plotted strategies to free those left behind.

Over the course of eleven years, she led more than thirteen expeditions, leading about seventy people to freedom herself and indirectly helping sixty others. Her long story is full of suffering and danger but also miracles and glory. Her life is still an inspiration. Tubman's conviction that she was fulfilling a purpose greater than herself was her driving force that moved her to leadership, even against all the challenges that opposed her.

Leadership is not easy when society opposes you because of gender, race, social status, or physical conditions. But the key to overcoming any opposition is to know that it is God who calls.

Like Tubman, Deborah led her people in a time of great social and political upheaval. Her personal status did not facilitate the recognition or exercise of that leadership. But she kept her eyes on the One who called her, careful to give all the glory to God.

Leadership challenges are a reminder that we have been called to fulfill a purpose beyond ourselves.

—MARY ANN MARTÍNEZ

TODAY

List the challenges you face and how they help you fulfill your calling.

LIVING GOD'S PERSPECTIVE

My ears had heard of you but now my eyes have seen you. (Job 42:5)

Sometimes we collide head-on with our human frailties, limitations, and imperfections. It is then, when we recognize our humanness, that we begin to see a glimpse of God's abundant grace.

God also sees you; whoever you are, wherever you are, whatever your life situation, you are not invisible to him. Against all opposition, God is going to set the conditions so that you can fulfill his purpose. The call that God has given you does not expire; it does not get canceled when circumstances change. Embrace the call with joy, courage, and faithfulness.

In the fulfillment of that higher calling, you would think everything would go smoothly. But the reality is that life is going to hit you with twists and turns. Never forget that God is always in, by, and above every one of them. You are his, and nothing happens to you by chance. You are sowing for eternity.

Just keep going; God will not forsake you.

PRAYER

Lord, thank you for all that brings joy to my life; help me enjoy it. When anxiety rushes me to decisions, please quiet my spirit. Help me face the challenges of the call you have placed in my hands. In the name of Jesus, Amen.

REV. DR. MARY ANN MARTÍNEZ
is a writer, psychotherapist, and ordained minister of the Church of God (Anderson) [USA]. She has been working in pastoral ministry and the mental health field for more than thirty years. She lives in Puerto Rico with her husband and her two dogs.

CALLED TO THINK AND SPEAK

ANOINTED TO PROCLAIM THE GOOD NEWS

"The Spirit of the Lord is on me, because he has anointed me
to proclaim good news to the poor." (Luke 4:18)

One Sunday, I was given the privilege to preach. The church had several pastors, and I was one of two female preachers on staff. As I began the introduction of the sermon, I noticed a couple of young men stand up and walk out; they could not hold their discontent and expressed their disapproval of seeing a woman preaching from the pulpit by simply walking out.

My heart sank! I had never experienced such obvious rejection. I tried to compose myself, but my nerves had the best of me. All I wanted to do was run away from that place as fast as I could. I didn't know how I would be able to find the necessary strength to continue, but the Holy Spirit brought a sense of confirmation that it was God who anointed me to proclaim his Word and embraced me with his love and approval of what I was doing.

When you and I accept the calling to ministry, we may face rejection in different ways. But this should not minimize who we are or who God is in us. With a calling, God will give us the capacity to proclaim the Word and stand with confidence in who we are in Christ. After this incident, I made sure I would remember this possibility of rejection but also remember how to bounce back in the confidence of God's calling in my life.

—JOHANNA CHACÓN RUGH

TODAY

Be prepared to boldly proclaim what God has placed in your heart.

PROCLAIM FROM SCRIPTURE

For you have been born again, not of perishable seed, but of imperishable, through the living and enduring word of God. (1 Pet. 1:23)

Living and enduring! In this verse, these two words speak to an ongoing situation, describing a noun in the present tense. Yes, the Bible is the greatest book ever written; it has provided living and enduring wisdom through centuries. In it, we find a plethora of material for preaching. So why preach from different sources? After all, we have been called to proclaim the Word of God. Why is it sometimes easy to neglect to do this and settle for other types of material? To preach the Word, we need to meditate on it, think on it, and allow God's Word to preach to us, so that we can listen for what the Holy Spirit wants to say to us and through us.

One Sunday, I listened to a fellow pastor preach. Scripture was read at the beginning of the sermon, but several minutes passed and nothing of what the preacher was teaching about referred back to the text at the beginning. The sermon seemed to be focused on the preacher's eloquence and his wonderful family stories. In one of Eugene Peterson's well-known books, the late author reminded readers that as pastors, we preach of God's story! When I keep this in mind, it helps me remember that the sermon and preaching it are not about me, not about how I can fit my own agenda in; rather, it's about God. And the one thing that will help me see and understand God's story is the Word of God.

—JOHANNA CHACÓN RUGH

TODAY

Write down how God's Word speaks to you; be a scripture-centered preacher!

SHARE THE GOSPEL

Jesus went throughout Galilee, teaching in their synagogues, proclaiming the good news of the kingdom, and healing every disease and sickness among the people. (Matt. 4:23)

I grew up in the home of a passionate gospel preacher. I still remember the "crusades" my father organized to share the message of the Gospel. While we were living in Spain, one of the highlights was putting up a tent and inviting a gathering of people to sing and share a message. This had never been done in the little towns we were visiting. It was all new. Many people came to know Jesus during that time.

Evangelistic crusades have become a thing of the past; however, we still live in a world full of people eager to hear the message of hope. The reason Jesus went to different places proclaiming the good news is because people were looking for hope, for a good news message that would change their situation. Today is no different. There are still people longing to hear the good news.

The good news can be heard anywhere—from a pulpit, a conversation, a radio interview, or a waiter in a restaurant. We are heralds of the wonderful news of Jesus Christ. You and I can't keep the transforming message of the gospel inside. The Holy Spirit will direct our paths in such a way that God gives us plenty of opportunities to share his good news with everyone.

—JOHANNA CHACÓN RUGH

TODAY

Be a beacon of good news wherever you go today.

GRACE—CENTERED PREACHING

When he saw many of the Pharisees and Sadducees coming to where
he was baptizing, he said to them: "You brood of vipers!
Who warned you to flee from the coming wrath?" (Matt. 3:7)

When I heard the reports of a condescending sermon at one of our churches, my heart hurt for those who had attended the service that day. The sermon was used as a way for the preacher to express his anger and frustration at a recent situation the congregation had gone through. There were derogatory words expressed toward people who were no longer part of the congregation but still had family members there.

I have always wrestled with John the Baptist's expression, "You brood of vipers!" To me, it seemed harsh. I may not have totally immersed myself in his context; but today, we as preachers can be insensitive to those who are listening to our preaching.

Let's remember that we enjoy the benefit of living by the grace of Jesus Christ. It's for this reason I want to make sure I not only enjoy and live in the reality of grace but also season my preaching with the same grace God has given me. And it must be expressed in my preaching. Our goal as preachers is to constantly remind our community of God's grace. We are living in a world where the enemy is taking advantage of every failure by Christians, making Christians feel their unworthiness. That is a great reason for me and you to continue reminding our hearers of the grace of Jesus Christ.

—JOHANNA CHACÓN RUGH

TODAY

Identify God's grace in your life today; share this grace with others.

WORLD—CONSCIOUS PREACHING

When Jesus landed and saw a large crowd, he had compassion on them, because they were like sheep without a shepherd. So he began teaching them many things. (Mark 6:34)

I love how the preacher at my church each Sunday reminds the congregation, "You are not just dismissed, you are sent!" after the benediction. Yes, sent to a world that is desperately waiting to receive compassion from our hearts. The reason the preacher says, "you are sent" is because the sermon reminds the congregation how each member can be light and salt in the world outside of church.

Dr. David Ward writes poignantly in *Practicing the Preaching Life* about the importance of aiming our preaching so that it is "something that benefits the world, not only the church." He advises preachers "not merely to delight the listener, but to move a worshiping community out into the world."

Our preaching must take into account those who are still outside the building. The way we do this is by preaching in a way that relates and empathizes with what those in the world are going through. When we read in Mark's account of how Jesus *felt*, the word *compassion* should move us to understand that this is how Christ wants us to respond to those in the world: as though they are sheep without a shepherd. The way we do that is by preaching the gospel with connections to our own situations. In this way, our preaching helps the hearers relate to the needs of those who are in our neighborhoods and in the world.

—JOHANNA CHACÓN RUGH

TODAY

Remember, your preaching is preparing your people to engage with the world.

SPEAKING WITH CONVICTION

Then Deborah said to Barak, "Go! This is the day the LORD has given Sisera into your hands. Has not the LORD gone ahead of you?" (Judg. 4:14)

I know a pastoral couple the Holy Spirit gifts with words of wisdom and prophecy. I must admit, at the beginning, I was skeptical about their gift. But God has used them in powerful ways to bring words of wisdom to his people. One important quality about their words is the sense of anointed conviction with which they speak. When they speak, they share wisdom they are certain comes from God's own heart, and I along with many others can testify the words are true.

When Deborah encouraged Barak, she knew God was speaking through her. The boldness and conviction with which she spoke is what encouraged Barak to go and fight that battle against Sisera. In the same way, remember that God can use me and you to be God's voice of encouragement to someone who needs to hear those words to fight their battles!

The more you and I spend time in God's presence, the easier it is to hear and discern the voice of the Holy Spirit and to be certain the words being given to us are from God's own heart. Not all of us may have the gift of prophecy, but all of us have been given the opportunity, through the Holy Spirit, to sense God's voice and to speak words that will make an impact in the lives of those eager to hear God speak through you.

—JOHANNA CHACÓN RUGH

TODAY

Practice speaking boldly when the Holy Spirit nudges you.

SHAPING A POSTURE TOWARD PREACHING

And the God of all grace, who called you to his eternal glory in Christ,
after you have suffered a little while, will himself restore you and
make you strong, firm and steadfast. (1 Pet. 5:10)

For the last six days, I've shared my posture toward preaching, my life experiences, and convictions. I have resolved that my preaching should be Bible-centered, grace-centered, and world-conscious. I should be able to preach with boldness and to edify the Church by the proclamation of the gospel of Jesus Christ from my own perspective and contextualize it in my own setting to produce transformation over time in the lives of those who hear.

This is what I believe; I cannot impose my theology of preaching on you. God has created us uniquely and differently to be a blessing to his Church, the Body of Christ. But my hope is that you are encouraged to shape your own approach to preaching, your own theology of proclamation, speaking with the confidence of Christ in you.

I grew up reading the Spanish 1960 Revised Version of the Bible, similar to the English New King James, which renders our text with a different emphasis that I would like to share with you in our prayer.

PRAYER

Father, thank you for the privilege of serving you in building and encouraging
your people through preaching. I ask you to continue perfecting, establishing,
strengthening, and settling us for the task you have called us to do. Amen.

REV. JOHANNA CHACÓN RUGH
is an ordained minister and serves The Wesleyan Church as director of Spanish
Ministry, Education, and Clergy Care as well as director of Thrive Financial Initiative
for Education & Clergy Development. In this role, Johanna serves alongside a team
of Hispanic leaders providing direction and support to Hispanic ministerial students.
Johanna, her husband, Robert, and family make their home in Fishers, Indiana, USA.

TELL THEM THEY ARE CLAIMED

For this reason I kneel before the Father, from whom every family
in heaven and on earth derives its name. (Eph. 3:14–15)

It wasn't all that long ago that I walked down a church hallway and found someone calling out to me with a familiar sparkle in his eyes. "Ah, now this one is one of my own!" His words felt like a warm embrace. His hair held more grey than it used to. The corners of the pastor's smile were now generously layered with lines from years of smiles shared—like the layers of prayers he had prayed for me. No doubt he lifted me up by name to a God who knew my name. In season and out, he reminded me I was someone worth claiming. For me—raised without a dad—the tender love of God's people has often stood in the gaps of my own story.

All around me today there are young people wanting more than anything to simply be someone's own. I nurture a child's faith when I dare to be someone safe, someone who knows their name and speaks their name with joy. It isn't always my lessons or my programs that make the most impact: sometimes kids and youth simply need to know they are known.

As a pastor now myself, I'm aware my smiles and words speak volumes over young people in my care. God uses me to root them in a faith-family steeped in the love of God who claims us. You and I are both recipients and extenders of this life-altering love.

—AISLING ZWEIGLE

TODAY

Speak Triune love over a young person; remind them they're claimed.

TELL THEM ABOUT THE HOPE OF THE HOLY SPIRIT

I pray that out of his glorious riches he may strengthen you with power
through his Spirit in your inner being. (Eph. 3:16)

I was sitting again in a church covered with a tin roof. The sun shone bright and hot, making sweat serve as air conditioning for the day. Roosters crowed outside. The smell of smoke trailed in as small trash heaps burned. Humble offerings of fish and rice were prepared in an adjacent room. Young people were telling me in their own words what it was like to be sponsored children at the child development centers in the Philippines. They are grown now, but their stories still inspire me today.

Growing up in the slums, these young people were told by many voices that they wouldn't amount to anything. The legacy of their loved ones often included addiction and poverty, dead ends and broken stories. These stories loomed like tall, dark shadows. But the Holy Spirit was on the move too—and the Spirit's power is more glorious than the shadows.

The Holy Spirit is able to shine brighter than a hot tin roof on a sunny day. The Spirit's work gives everyone the power to overcome the deep darkness. The Spirit teaches traumatized hearts to hope.

Whether you grew up in a tin-roof shack or a two-story home, the Holy Spirit is more than able to strengthen you to hope, learn, and lead.

—AISLING ZWEIGLE

TODAY

Seek the Spirit's presence in your inner being, speaking the impossible.

TELL THEM CHRIST IS AT HOME WITH THEM

So that Christ may dwell in your hearts through faith. (Eph. 3:17)

She looked up at me with her big eyes. Sitting on the front row of our children's church gathering, she asked me, "What does it mean to dwell?" Sometimes we grown-ups use fancy words, while kids are often waiting for us to speak their language—to make scripture come alive in a way that curls up next to them in their bunkbeds at night while they pray. Their eyes are begging us to make the promises of Jesus come so close to their everyday lives that they can laugh next to Jesus on the playground while they play.

The book of Ephesians helps us discover exactly this kind of nearness to Christ, as he dwells in our hearts. The key to unlock it is faith. We can remind young people that as they put their faith in Jesus, they allow the power of Christ's love to make such a difference in their story that Jesus moves in and makes his home in their hearts. Not a fancy home with linens on the table, where no guests get past the outer formal space. No, Paul was writing about a love that gets so deep in our lives, it swings its legs over the side of the couch, takes its socks off, and tells stories late into the night.

How does Jesus dwell in you?

—AISLING ZWEIGLE

TODAY

Allow Christ to make himself at home with you.

SHOW THEM HOW FAR GRACE WILL TRAVEL

I pray that you, being rooted and established in love, may . . . grasp how wide and long and high and deep is the love of Christ. (Eph. 3:17–18)

When children hear I've run marathons, often they ask me if I won! They don't always understand the sheer volume of people who run in a race. Similarly, when children know a loved one is traveling far away, it's challenging for them to comprehend the distance. Parents might measure time in number of "sleeps," or whatever it takes to make a unit of something familiar—something that makes space, or time, or a race make sense.

I remember being told about the grace of Christ as a young person. It sounded extravagant. Then, I encountered a moment when the grace of Jesus came alive.

My friends wanted me to take things that weren't mine, sneak out of the house, and then give the things away. So, taking my powers of strategic thinking, I went rogue—then wrote all about it in a note my mom found. Big trouble.

But instead of trouble, I encountered big love. I cried tears of remorse. My mom spoke to me about who I was and how these actions didn't reflect that person. Instead of pulling away, she came closer. She showed me the distance grace travels, using units of measurement I understood.

To this day, when someone talks about the extravagant grace of Jesus, I remember the love of my mother that night. She took what was abstract, the width and length and height and depth of Christ's love, and put skin on it.

—AISLING ZWEIGLE

TODAY

Bring the love of Christ to life; measure with loving action.

SHOW THEM HOW TO LOOK FOR GOD

Know this love that surpasses knowledge—that you may be filled to
the measure of all the fullness of God. (Eph. 3:19)

It was a breezy day on the beach in Vancouver, British Columbia, Canada. Hordes of people enjoyed much-awaited warmth and sunshine. My young boys were in the sea of people. They made tide-pool discoveries. Their eyes looked down with delight. Soon they were far away. To my eyes, they were like small dots of color on a canvas. They never left my line of vision; they were always in my care. But their eyes were on everything but me.

In a moment, my oldest son's perspective radically changed. He looked up in search of me. I could see panic flashing through him. It's possible to feel very alone in a crowd when you're afraid. I waved my hands. I hurried to get near him and pull him to myself. The relief he felt was visceral; it probably reached his fingertips and toes. He was never lost, but the fullness of love watching over him was well beyond his knowledge!

As a leader, have you found yourself in a place filled with people and activities grasping for your attention? These may include delightful things and hard things that stretch your own capacity. Before you know it, you find yourself out at sea without any certainty that God still has you. It's possible to feel incredibly alone and afraid in an overwhelming place. Even in this place, the Lord's love can be found: it surpasses your knowledge but fills you still.

—AISLING ZWEIGLE

TODAY

Stop what you're doing and look for the Lord.

TELL THEM ABOUT GOD'S IMMEASURABLE TRUSTWORTHINESS

Now to him who is able to do immeasurably more than all we ask or imagine, according to his power that is at work within us . . . (Eph. 3:20)

What's the wildest dream you've ever had while you were asleep? When I was a young child, I used to have a recurring dream that I could fly. Even now, the thought makes me smile.

However, when I was a child, this dream started as a stress dream, stemming from one of the most traumatic experiences I had as a young child. I saw the scene play out in my mind, but the ending was different; I could simply fly away. A dream that started in reaction to trauma shifted to become a favorite moment, the dream ending with a feeling of freedom and joy in flying, flapping arms and all. In this, "immeasurably more" than I could ever hope became the Spirit's power at work within me.

I'm convinced that some of the Spirit's greatest work in our lives and in our world is in the very places that have been deemed most unreachable. This is true for children-at-risk who have experienced trauma. This is true for wandering young people living outside of God's hope. And this is true for us as we face obstacles in our faith-families, where wounds are used as weapons of harm, not help. There is still need for a journey of healing. But we continue to find joy in flying: God is able to do immeasurably more!

—AISLING ZWEIGLE

TODAY

Entrust a hard thing to God's goodness; expect God's very best work!

SHOW THEM GOOD-HUMORED HUMILITY

To him be glory in the church and in Christ Jesus throughout
all generations, for ever and ever! Amen. (Eph. 3:21)

The banquet was ready, the room full of well-dressed, hungry people deciding which table to join. Once the guests were all seated, we did the work of getting acquainted with our tablemates. When the host holding the microphone stepped onto the stage, he spoke over the hum of light conversation. Thanking everyone for coming, he explained that the guest speaker and spouse were invited to be first in line for food. My husband and I arched our necks to look around the room; so did everyone else. It was at this moment we realized everyone was looking at us. It seems that we were apparently "the guest speaker and spouse"! Something definitely got lost in translation when we were invited to come to the event.

As humorous as it was, at the time it was also quite stressful. Ministry holds surprises. There are times we miss an important memo (that was never written). If every moment is about looking our best, then "sweating bullets" is not a good place to start! Thankfully, every moment is actually an opportunity for God's glory—not ours—so we're off the hook.

PRAYER

Lord Jesus, teach us to turn our trust toward you, whatever the day holds. Teach us to seek your glory in all we do. When we are humbled, enliven our spirits to see how your power takes center stage and transforms each moment. Amen.

REV. AISLING ("ASHLING") ZWEIGLE

is an ordained elder in the Church of the Nazarene. She is the family life pastor at Tenth Church, a multisite congregation in Vancouver, British Columbia, a congregation in the Christian and Missionary Alliance Church of Canada. She has held a variety of positions with churches and nonprofit organizations, including children's pastor, children and families pastor, and early childhood educator. Aisling is married to Dr. Grant Zweigle; they have two awesome boys in university.

JUST TAKE A SIP

But whoever drinks the water I give them will never thirst. (John 4:14)

The dust in her eyes and the sun beating down were still a better option than the morning trek. The glares and glances, whispers and obvious avoidance were more than she could handle. Beat down, worn out, soul-thirsty, heart-hopeless, needing water, she walked by herself to a well that offered the fulfillment of very few of her needs. Caught off guard, she saw a man, a Jew. *Turn around? Wait. What did he say? A drink? What kind of water?*

Did you know that the woman at the well was the first to hear Jesus' confession that he was the Messiah? Each of us prepares "the word of God for the people of God," often knowing more than we want to about most of those very people. Sometimes they are dried up and thirsty, skeptical, beaten down, hopeless, and here we are by a well with living water asking them to drink. *Please, just take a sip.*

Jesus knew this woman. He had the inside scoop on a dried-up life and instead of preaching at her, he invited her company. It's easy to fall into a kind of "just cut it out!" preaching category, allowing our knowledge to tinge the way we preach to the flock we know. Instead, this week, whoever your people are, in whatever setting, look at them with new eyes. Ask God for a heart of compassion and confession. Ask yourself, "How can I invite them, with open arms, to drink the living water of Jesus?"

—RACHEL A. KUHN

TODAY

Go out of your way to offer a physical drink to someone.

HEART STRINGS

For the word of God is alive and active. (Heb. 4:12)

She stood from her seat, gliding across the platform. Every eye was on her, and the jam-packed convention center fell to a hush as we watched her maneuver into position. The strings stretched from floor to ceiling: an enormous earth harp. As she played each string, I lost myself in song. My heart had never resonated so much with the blend of music and motion as I sat and took in my first earth harp experience.

Years later, I stood on a platform of a different sort. Staring up at me were faces I knew and recognized. I was their pastor; they were my people. Each of their hearts and lives had attached to mine like the earth harp strings. I felt the slack, the tension, the vibrations, the stillness of their walks with Jesus, each written sermon becoming a song that resonated deeply with my heart and theirs.

This living, breathing, active word of God connects itself to each of us, but it also connects us to each other, creating an earth-to-heavens harp that plays the music of our souls. As we bring this word to our people, we must be faithful to the whole, conditioning ourselves to know the strings so that the heart of God is revealed and the people of God are transformed. We will only find this if we give our will and desired outcomes over to the Word who actively writes the song.

—RACHEL A. KUHN

 TODAY

Begin to memorize Hebrews 4:12.

IMPOSSIBLE DIRT

Still other seed fell on good soil, where it produced a crop—a hundred,
sixty or thirty times what was sown. (Matt. 13:8)

We topped the mountain and piled out of the taxi onto dry Andes dirt. The heat hit us along with the odor from outhouses that lined the hillside. To my left was a graveyard with plots much too small to hold anyone who should be buried there. Dust and dirt clung to our shoes as we made our way to the little church. Then, like the sun on a cloudy day, out popped bright, shining children's faces. They were wearing the only clothes they had, preparing to eat the one balanced meal they would receive that week. Pastora Susanna baked in an outdoor kitchen while the group told stories and played games. Each child, even the smallest, was on their own, while parents worked long hard days in the city.

When it was time to leave, our exit was heart-wrenching. In tears, I confessed to God, "There is just too much: too much death, hunger, poverty, hopelessness." Then God responded with a few simple words: "Rachel, this is good soil and the seed planted here will produce a crop that is one hundred times what has been planted." And so it was. Ten years later, that community is thriving. God and his church transformed that little place. Pastor, never underestimate what God can do in what looks like impossible dirt!

—RACHEL A. KUHN

TODAY

Look at a field and contemplate the harvest.

BATHROBES AND CIGARETTES

Now there was a Pharisee, a man named Nicodemus who was a member
of the Jewish ruling council. He came to Jesus at night. (John 3:1–2)

I grew up in a small town in the southern part of West Virginia. My home church was just around the bend from what is now the New River Gorge National Park. The people of West Virginia are proud and strong-willed, with even stronger bonds. Their love for one another runs deep and their ties to their culture are nearly unbreakable. Even after twenty years of living outside the Appalachia region, my accent can still go "from zero to cornbread" in two and a half seconds.

Growing up, I joked that if anyone from church smoked, they did it under their back porch at night in their bathrobe so no one would ever know. There were a few old church ladies that pulled it off seamlessly.

Jesus and Nicodemus met. There may not have been bathrobes or cigarettes, but there was a blanket of darkness and a deep-seated culture that needed light. Jesus met Nicodemus where he was and shed light on his darkness. I love how Jesus loves us right where are but loves us way too much to leave us there.

Jesus battled darkness and cultural hurdles with the truth of the light of God. We too have that ability, if we will stop for a minute, look at those around us, and be willing to meet them with the light of God right in the middle of their darkness.

—RACHEL A. KUHN

TODAY

Stand outside in the dark, light a flame, and watch it burn.

SPEAK LiFE

Then he said to me, "Prophesy to these bones and say to them,
'Dry bones, hear the word of the LORD!'" (Ezek. 37:4)

As with most major prophets, the calling of Ezekiel was not fair and not hope-filled. At thirty years old, he should have been stepping into his priestly role and serving in the temple. Instead, he was living the life of an exile. He longed for what could be, instead of what was reality.

We all know the story of hope that lies in this chapter. God transports Ezekiel from his home to a valley filled with death and dried-up old bones. God commands Ezekiel to speak a prophetic word, and out of his lips flow words of life. Bones start rattling and join together with tendons and flesh. Then breath comes from the four winds and gives life to an army. God declares victory even over death.

God could have done this all on his own. He could have taken Ezekiel to the valley and told the bones what to do and reaffirmed his power in front of the prophet. But that's not how God did it. God called Ezekiel and gave him the words to say. God brought life from his lips. And so it is with you, sister. God has called you. God has given you a word for his people. God will bring life from your lips. Listen for God's voice and be brave in the valley. Trust God. Then, preach it, sister!

—RACHEL A. KUHN

TODAY

Speak a word of encouragement to a stranger.

GET OUT OF THE WAY

"Who was I to think that I could stand in God's way?" (Acts 11:17)

"Don't smoke or chew or go with girls who do." This was the "deep," slightly misguided mantra of my youth group days. If we stayed far away from bad habits and clung tightly to those who did right, then we might make it to heaven!

Peter stood before the apostles. I imagine they looked something like headmasters glaring over the rims of their round wire glasses. In a declaration affirming their beliefs, they confronted Peter with his transgressions. How dare he eat in the home of an uncircumcised gentile! What was Peter's response? "Who was I to think I could stand in God's way?"

It is an overwhelming task to sit with the Word of God, wanting and waiting and praying for it to open up like a sheet filled with transformational revelation for us and our people. Then when it does, often we look at what is inside and say, "Never mind! Lord, I can't preach that." We stumble over questions and concerns, confrontations we are sure to face if we unfold the Word in a way that provokes the religious. In the end, it is not our job to please the religious but to preach the revelation.

Ladies, are you struggling with any thoughts or mindsets that are standing in the way of what God wants to do? Take a moment and give those over to God today.

—RACHEL A. KUHN

TODAY

Step out of God's way.

i DO

"I have come to bring fire on the earth, and how
I wish it were already kindled!" (Luke 12:49)

Tears filled my eyes, as they do every time I hear the ordination liturgy read. In my heart, I affirm the words again and again, more powerfully each year. As time lengthens, so does my passion for the vows I took years ago. I was fifteen years old when the call came to me on a mission trip in Wyoming, and now I live it out in Ohio. It has taken me on a journey of faithfulness with beautiful and necessary stops along the way. If it's been a while, encourage your heart by rereading your denominational ordination liturgy.

Something about preaching "the Word of God to the people of God" ignites in me an insatiable fire. Passion flows like lava, igniting all in its path. But that isn't me. It is a mixture of the spark already in me, the wind of God that ignites it, and the accelerant of the Holy Spirit that creates a transformational word. Sister, you are called. You have a spark. Open up your heart and mind and watch God light up the world.

PRAYER

Oh God, today grant my sister passion for your Word, hope for her people, and light to ignite her path. May she proclaim your Word with truth and authenticity, resting in your goodness and grace, today and always. Amen.

REV. RACHEL A. KUHN

serves as lead pastor at the Tipp City Church of the Nazarene in Ohio, and as East Central Field Women's Clergy Representative for the Church of the Nazarene, USA. Rachel has four children, serves as a foster parent, and enjoys reading, traveling, being outdoors, and spending time with family.

CALLED TOGETHER

GOD'S LOVE THROUGH GOD'S PEOPLE

Surely your goodness and love will follow me all the days of my life. (Ps. 23:6)

My sisters and I were living in the Texas Rio Grande valley when our parents decided we were traveling to Idaho for the summer. All the girl cousins jumped in the back of my uncle's mattress-lined potato truck. We talked, giggled, slept, and ate bologna sandwiches for two days. We arrived at a labor camp made up of dilapidated one-room shacks, outhouses, and community showers. We woke at dawn to work in the sugar beet fields. We found joy in talking and laughing as we raced our cousins to see who would be the first to finish weeding their rows. On weekends, our uncles would kill and roast a *cabrito* (goat), our aunts would prepare rice and beans, and the cousins would play until it was time to feast.

In Psalm 23, David reminds us that the Good Shepherd is faithful in his guidance, provision, justice, and refreshment. That summer, a small Hispanic Pentecostal church welcomed our family. People from the church told my parents about local jobs and invited us into their homes. We did not return to Texas with our cousins.

The farmworker community is a beautiful, resilient, and proud community. But they still face unfair labor practices, inadequate housing, and immigration barriers. God wants his Church to provide pastures of provision, tables of belonging, and refuge from injustice for his sheep. A good shepherd cares about everything that impacts the health and well-being of his sheep.

—HERMINIA ESQUEDA

TODAY

Create spaces of provision, belonging, and refuge for God's sheep.

SHE WASHED MY FEET

"For even the Son of Man did not come to be served, but to serve,
and to give his life as a ransom for many." (Mark 10:45)

My *suegra* (mother-in-law) lived with my family for twenty-one years until she passed away at the age of one hundred. When she moved in with us, my daughter Brianna was two years old. I remember my *suegra* saying, *"No me voy a ingrir, porque me voy a morir"* ("I am not getting close to her because I am going to die"). But her plan failed. Brianna and her *abuelita* had *café con leche* (coffee with milk) and *pan dulce* (sweet bread) every morning. Soon, Brianna was brushing her *abuelita*'s hair and helping her thread sewing needles. One evening my *suegra* came to me and my husband in tears. *"¡La niña! ¡La niña!"* ("The child! The girl!") We thought something had happened to Brianna, but through her tears, she said, *"Me lavó los pies."* ("She washed my feet.")

Jesus spent time with those who lived on the margins—the poor, the sick, the outcast, women and children. On the eve of his death, Jesus chose to wash his disciples' feet. It was a reminder to the disciples that we are not called to be served but to serve.

No amount of intelligence, athletic ability, or money could impress my mother-in-law. But to wash someone else's feet? Now that was the ultimate demonstration of humility, love, and sacrifice. Whose feet are you called to wash that would require your love, humility, and sacrifice?

—HERMINIA ESQUEDA

TODAY

Serve those around you with love, humility, and sacrifice.

SEEING WITH THE EYES OF GOD WHO SEES ME

She gave this name to the LORD who spoke to her:
"You are the God who sees me." (Gen. 16:13)

As I was getting off a plane at an airport, I noticed an *abuelita* (grandmother) traveling alone. From a distance, I kept my eye on her as she walked briskly down the "C" corridor and approached three separate airport attendants, who all appeared to dismiss her. I ran to catch up to her and asked, *"¿Le puedo ayudar?"* ("Can I help you?") She said there was no gate number on her boarding pass. I looked up her flight and walked her to her gate at the far end of the "D" corridor. We discovered that we both travel a lot to visit our children and grandchildren. I asked her if she was ever afraid of traveling alone. She smiled and confidently said, *"No. Dios siempre me trae un ángel para ayudarme."* ("No. God always brings me an angel to help me.") We hugged and went our separate ways. I left encouraged by her *abuelita* faith.

The Lord heard Hagar's affliction and made himself known. Hagar, in return, gave God the name *El Roi*, "the God who sees me." The *abuelita* at the airport reminded me of Hagar. She knew, without a doubt, that "the God who sees me" would bring someone to help her in her time of need. Who are the *abuelitas* in your community who go unseen or dismissed? We may be surprised at what we can learn from listening to and learning from the voices of the unseen.

—HERMINIA ESQUEDA

TODAY

Identify, listen, and learn from the *abuelitas* around you.

BECAUSE CHRIST LOVED US FIRST

When Jesus landed and saw a large crowd, he had compassion on them,
because they were like sheep without a shepherd. (Mark 6:34)

In 2018, when my social media feed was covered with opinions about the asylum seekers headed north from Central America, the posts from churches in Mexico looked drastically different. There were images and videos of churches joining together to feed, clothe, shelter, and offer medical assistance. In one day, the Church in poverty-stricken Mexico literally fed 5,000 travelers. The image that stands out in my memory is the joy on everyone's faces, both the givers and the recipients. One grateful recipient stated that beyond material assistance that quickly fades, he will always remember everyone's kindness and friendship that never fades.

In our text, Jesus saw the multitudes and was moved with compassion. The disciples, knowing they only had five loaves of bread and two fish, were of the opinion that the crowds should be sent away. But Jesus' compassion moved him to action. After they ate, he sent the disciples ahead of him and Jesus stayed with the crowd. Jesus' actions always included relationship.

The Spirit moved the Church in Mexico. Their compassion moved them to action. Like Jesus, their action included love, kindness, and relationship. When one of the helpers was asked why they were doing what they did, she responded, "Because Christ loved us first and has called us to love our neighbor." Who are the multitudes in your neighborhood who are suffering? Ask the Holy Spirit to move you and your congregation with compassion that is followed by action and relationship.

—HERMINIA ESQUEDA

TODAY

Be moved with compassion, followed by action and relationship.

WHO iS MY NEiGHBOR?

But a Samaritan, as he traveled, came where the man was; and when he saw him, he took pity on him. (Luke 10:33)

A few years ago, my friend Becky and I started meeting early on Monday mornings for discipleship. Our studies always ended with discussions on how the Church can make a difference against the suffering and injustices of the world. Becky shared how her father, a pastor, had agreed to sponsor two young men from Haiti who were being held at a detention center in Texas. The young men had written to every church in the area thinking, "Certainly there are brothers and sisters in Christ who will help us."

Their prayers were answered through a small immigrant church in Washington State. Becky's church supported these young men financially, found employment for them, and drove them to their immigration appointments. Every week I got to listen to stories of their beautiful and challenging journey. I attended one of their church services one evening; one of the Haitian young men was preaching in French, the second young man was translating to Spanish, and a third person was translating to English. It was beautiful!

In Jesus' parable, he elevates the voice of the Samaritan by making him the hero of the story. He describes a neighbor as one who gives sacrificially to care for the physical needs of the suffering. The immigrant church was a good neighbor when they gave sacrificially and elevated the voices of their Haitian brothers.

Who are the ostracized in your community? How will you elevate their voices or be their neighbor?

—HERMiNiA ESQUEDA

TODAY

Go and do likewise.

LIViNG iN COMMUNiTY

All the believers were together and had everything in common. (Acts 2:44)

I meet with a group of *pastoras* (women clergy) who gather to learn about the immigration crisis and the church. I am supposed to be their leader, but I have been the learner. As I share academic research and the history of immigration, they share their lived experience. They share stories of racism, dehumanization, fear of deportation, and the daily struggles faced by their congregations. It has been beautiful to witness how these *hermanas* (sisters) lift each other up, pray for one another, share resources, and brainstorm solutions. They live and love in community.

After Pentecost, the church of Acts was devoted to two things: the apostles' teaching and fellowship. They learned together, ate together, and prayed together. Like the church in Acts, the beautiful *pastoras* in my small group are anointed women of God. They are devoted to learning, growing, and praying for one another.

As we focus on our ministry, our calling, our gifts, our purpose, and our personal relationship with God, our faith can become very individualistic. The church of Acts was never about one individual. It was their unity that amazed those around them. We can learn so much from our *hermanas* who live in community. They know we are better together. How can we grow our faith and our ministry in community? How can we be less individualistic and more kingdom-minded?

—HERMiNiA ESQUEDA

TODAY

Seek out diverse voices and perspectives that live in community.

LET JUSTICE FLOW DOWN

But let justice roll on like a river, righteousness like a never-failing stream! (Amos 5:24)

Last year I met a friend online who was grieved by the racial unrest in our country and was asking for resources. I responded and we quickly found others equally grieved and struggling with next steps. We formed a network of bridge-builders across the country who have been listening, learning, and growing together. What I didn't expect was to find a sisterhood of strong women clergy from diverse backgrounds and perspectives whose friendship was a healing balm to my soul. We shared how lonely this work feels sometimes and how grateful we are to have each other.

We were able to listen firsthand to the pain and injustices impacting our Black brothers and sisters. We wept as we listened to the stories of racist attacks against the elderly in Asian communities. We saw God open doors to partner with immigrant resource agencies. We prayed for the challenges we face in each of our local contexts. Proximity and relationship created a Holy Spirit bond of solidarity and mutuality. This is the Church!

PRAYER

You are the God who sees
Heal me from my blindness
You are the God who serves
Help me to give sacrificially
You are the God who comforts
Help me to weep with those who weep

PASTOR HERMINIA ESQUEDA

resides in Sunnyside, Washington, USA, and serves as an associate pastor and multicultural coordinator for the Northwest District Church of the Nazarene. Herminia has been in ministry for seven years after working in social services for over thirty years. She has three children, six grandchildren, and two great-grandchildren.

WHAT'S YOUR MOTTO?

Righteousness and justice are the foundation of your throne;
love and faithfulness go before you. (Ps. 89:14)

At the height of the COVID-19 pandemic, few churches gathered in person. However, this one did, and I was visiting on behalf of the district. The co-pastors were loved but were predictably dealing with tensions that had developed over the wearing of masks.

Songs were sung with heartfelt worship; then, it was someone's turn to give announcements. If I had not been there to witness what came next, I wouldn't have believed how quickly the group dynamics crashed and burned. It was awful. The woman at the microphone made an announcement about a meeting, to which someone shouted that the day was wrong. She sharply quipped that she only read what was written down. Back and forth it went, until the pastor took the microphone, saying, "Grace and mercy. That is our motto. Grace and mercy."

No sooner had those words come out of her mouth when the person in the sound booth came up and forcefully took the microphone out of the pastor's hand to explain how the day for the meeting was decided. Somehow, the pastor soon had the microphone again, and with a smile repeated, "Grace and mercy. That is our motto. Grace and mercy."

She probably needed the motto as much as anyone would in that moment! I was amazed at the wisdom she had for establishing a motto that she could use as a default posture in such a charged moment. As I left church, I took her motto with me (and soon needed it at my next family gathering).

—ANITA EASTLACK

TODAY

Lay a foundational motto as your default for times of tension.

CONSULT THE MANUAL

Love and faithfulness meet together; righteousness and
peace kiss each other. (Ps. 85:10)

I dreaded daylight saving time. It meant I would have to change the clock in my unfamiliar car. After two years of hassle, I finally checked the owner's manual: turns out, it was easy.

As preachers, we point people to the Bible as our manual for life. How do we facilitate love and faithfulness, allowing "righteousness and peace to kiss each other," when Christians don't even agree on many issues?

In Matthew 19, Jesus was asked to give a ruling on a moral dispute. He pointed people back to the "manual," the Holy Scriptures. Not only that, Jesus acknowledged our creator God as the authority. "Haven't you read, . . . " (his emphasis is applicable today) "that at the beginning the Creator 'made . . .'" (v. 4). Jesus went on to settle the debate. Our creator God established what is right and what is out of alignment. We are equipped when we trace our questions back to our creator God. Haven't you read . . . ?

The pace of our world and the change it brings can be overwhelming; but while modern labels are not the same labels used in the Bible, our challenges are not unique. There is nothing new under the sun. So how do we preach about justice and mercy in a world that seems as though it has been turned upside down? Follow Jesus' example and start at the beginning. Read how our creator God designed righteousness and peace to accompany each other.

—ANITA EASTLACK

TODAY

When you're overwhelmed by current events, begin at the beginning.

STEPPING INTO THE STREAM OF JUSTICE

But let justice roll on like a river, righteousness like a never-failing stream! (Amos 5:24)

I drove home from my visit with Springfield Wesleyan Church reflecting on God's justice that flows like a never-failing stream. Rev. Orange Scott is buried in Springfield, Massachusetts. He presided over the 1842 convention that organized The Wesleyan Methodist Connection. A passionate abolitionist, he preached that holy hearts should result in holy lives and that holy men should seek to bring an end to social evils such as slavery. His ministry was not easy; he was met with great opposition, but he willingly lived out his calling.

Today, there is a wonderful multiethnic Wesleyan church in Springfield, living out the calling of Orange Scott—that same congregation I visited. The pastor has been there for many years and has a "heart of gold." He grew up in rural America and came to a very different setting. Sometimes he finds bullet casings around the church grounds. In response, he mobilized some key leaders to be part of the city crime watch. In fact, they received an award for reducing crime in their urban neighborhood by 50 percent. A very small portion of his congregation is employed, yet every Saturday they extend generosity, inviting the neighborhood into their building for a much-needed home-cooked meal.

During my visit, before and after the service, I had several conversations and asked folks to share their stories. Some people were long-time attenders, others brand-new. Some came from deep brokenness and found transforming grace there; some grew up in the church. Together, they are truly a transforming presence.

—ANITA EASTLACK

TODAY

Get into the flowing river and see where God's justice takes you.

YOUR LEAST FAVORITE KIND OF PERSON

"Whatever you did for one of the least of these brothers and sisters
of mine, you did for me." (Matt. 25:40)

I finally conceded. My seven-year-old daughter, Rachel, begged until I agreed to buy her a hermit crab. I love animals, but a hermit crab is my least favorite. I made Rachel vow that I would never have to touch it; she would be responsible. Holding a pink cage and a container of food, she carefully listened to the storekeeper's instructions. Rachel strode out of the store with her head up, wearing a proud smile. Sadie the hermit crab was going home with us.

Rachel truly was responsible. I had no occasion to touch the creepy creature.

Two weeks after the visit to the pet store, Rachel uncharacteristically cried as she got into my sister's van, heading to camp. Why was she crying? I had a moment of doubt but still insisted that she get in, go, and have a good time.

I went into the house and carried on with my work while praying for Rachel to be all right. Why was she crying? I took laundry to my bedroom; sitting on my dresser was Sadie in her cage with the container of food and a note: "Mama, please take care of Sadie until I get home. Love, Rachel."

Suddenly, I loved Sadie, not because I love crabs, but because I love Rachel. Then, Matthew 25:40 washed over me: "Whatever you did for one of the least of these . . . you did for me." Yes, Jesus. I love you. I will love people—even the ones I have labeled "least"—because I love you.

—ANITA EASTLACK

TODAY

Show mercy to someone or something that makes you want to cringe.

MERCY IN THE TONE OF HUMILITY

And what does the LORD require of you? To act justly and to
love mercy and to walk humbly with your God. (Mic. 6:8)

I was surprised to find every seat filled; the prisoners were quietly waiting for the service to begin. One prisoner introduced herself to me as the choir and worship leader. She would lead first and then hand over the service to me. Worship began—loud, amazing, Spirit-filled. God's presence was sweet and intense and real.

For at least twenty minutes, my team and I wept in the front row as we worshiped with the women prisoners we thought we had come to teach. We had spent months preparing for this first visit to the women's prison. We were passionate about bringing love and mercy to women who needed Christ's message. Little did we know, we needed their message.

They loved God. They loved worship. Previously in their lives, they had done something wrong and ended up in prison. But as we had prepared for the visit, we had prepared as though they were all still far from God. We didn't think of ourselves as prideful as we got ready. But we also didn't know the whole story.

As my team and I shared, ministered, and encouraged, our message didn't change but our tone did. We shifted from teacher to sister, instructor to friend. We had prepared for the "act justly" and "love mercy" part of Micah 6:8 but surprisingly found "humility with your God" in prison.

—ANITA EASTLACK

TODAY

Assess and adjust your tone when you approach works of mercy.

THE HARDEST ONE TO SHOW MERCY

Blessed are the merciful, for they will be shown mercy. (Matt. 5:7)

If you are you like me, sometimes you may find that you are hardest on yourself. It has been a lifelong journey to heal and grow beyond criticizing myself internally. There are a multitude of reasons, from nature and nurture, for this inner battle. If I fall short or fall behind, I am prone to anxiety. My human nature internalizes the stress. Self-doubt soon engulfs me. Regrets accumulate.

The greatest commandment is familiar and usually taught in the context of loving others. Well established in my young Sunday school days was the practice of J-O-Y: to put *Jesus* first, *Others* second and *Yourself* last. It is just as useful for those of us who love others well but need to be reminded to be kind to ourselves. When we love our neighbor as we love our own selves, it opens the door for love to work more deeply in our own lives.

Next time you are running late for a meeting, falling behind, or falling short, extend the same grace to yourself that you would to others. The next time you preach and you don't feel great about it, let it roll off your shoulders and ask God to use it anyway. Praying the truth of Psalm 23 is a discipline that sets me free. When self-doubt begins to rise up within me, I pray with gratitude, "Surely goodness and love will follow me all the days of my life."

—ANITA EASTLACK

TODAY

Show yourself mercy just as you show mercy to others.

THE MERCY OF PRESENCE

I will betroth you in righteousness and justice, in love and compassion. (Hos. 2:19)

If you were to ask me the most extreme conditions I've ever experienced, I would say Sri Lanka after the 2004 tsunami and Haiti after the 2010 earthquake. Both were devastating beyond words or imagination.

In Sri Lanka, people were still in shock, eyes wide and walking robotically as we greeted them. We brought basic supplies and a time of ministry and prayer. The language barrier did not hinder the love that flowed through hugs, tears, and smiles as I listened to story after story of violent swirling water and the loss of loved ones and belongings. God's presence was precious. Surprisingly, the people responded to our visit as though it was somehow healing. As we hugged goodbye, the change in their physical demeanor was miraculous. They knew we cared. The gift of compassion and listening presence brought a measure of healing.

The same thing happened in Haiti. My team was warned not to engage the crowd at the airport begging as we walked to the van. "Avoid all eye contact!" I knew better than to pull out my wallet, but I knew I had to pull out my compassion. I looked into their eyes and smiled. They could not understand English but they returned my smile with their own big smiles. I gave what I could. They received it. They gave what they could. I received it.

PRAYER

Creator God, keep me close to the cross, remaining humble and hopeful. May my compass be Jesus' love, and my anchor, his unchanging truth. Holy Spirit, equip me to bring justice and mercy to all who bear your image. In Jesus' name. Amen.

REV. DR. ANITA EASTLACK
has been involved in ministry for forty years—twenty-nine of which have been spent in local church and district leadership. She has also served since 2016 as executive director of Church Multiplication and Discipleship for The Wesleyan Church. Anita grew up in a church-planting, multiethnic family, and she and her husband, Karl, are continuing that tradition.

ONE FAITH

Your kingdom come, your will be done, on earth as it is in heaven. (Matt. 6:10)

Shortly after leaving our first child—born at just twenty-four weeks—in the neonatal intensive care unit, my husband said to me, "If we really believe what the Bible says is true, then now is the time to start acting like it!" For me, that meant holding on to what the Spirit of God had told me weeks before my son was born: "He will live and not die."

In order to hold on to the faith those words inspired, I had to let go of the doctor's prognosis. I couldn't focus on how dire the circumstances looked for a one-pound, seven-ounce newborn facing heart surgery. Together, we focused on the Scripture and reminded ourselves of the promises of God. God intervened in our situation, and that baby boy is now twenty-one years old, a junior in college. In spite of the numerous struggles and challenges he faced, God has always been faithful. Now I apply that same principle to other areas of my life, especially ministry.

If you hope to create a transformative ministry in a diverse world, you must possess an audacious faith: one that dares to reimagine what is possible in our churches and our world. Only then will you be able to live a life that demonstrates to the world that you truly believe what the Bible says. You must believe that God is making all things new and that his kingdom will come.

—ROSHANDA AYANNA WOMACK

TODAY

Find two scripture verses about faith. Memorize one.

ONE FAMILY

Adam named his wife Eve, because she would become
the mother of all the living. (Gen. 3:20)

My mother is a Jamaican immigrant, and my father is African American with roots in West Africa. From birth, my parents wanted to make sure my siblings and I were aware of our cultural heritage. My father gave us all African names, and my mother made sure we developed a taste for all things Jamaican.

Having connections to our heritage gave us a sense of pride and belonging. It gave me a deeper understanding of the unique challenges minority groups like immigrants, people of color, and women face. It taught me the importance of listening and learning from people of different backgrounds. By listening to each other's stories, we learn that we are not nearly as different as we might think.

In Genesis 2, we find the story of God creating the first humans, Adam and Eve. If you're like me, you've probably read the creation story many times. But maybe you've never taken the time to consider the implications. If we believe God breathed life into humankind, that means we are all one human family. Learning about your cultural roots empowers you to embrace others. We are one family. Understanding this simple but profound truth is a key to developing ministries that transform all of humanity.

—ROSHANDA AYANNA WOMACK

TODAY

Nurture a relationship with someone from a different culture. Be teachable.

ONE PEOPLE

From one man he made all the nations,
that they should inhabit the whole earth. (Acts 17:26)

Have you ever considered why Africa is called the motherland? Archeologists call it the cradle of civilization; the oldest known fossils of *Homo sapiens* have been found there. Scripture serves to give us the proper context for considering the origins of our universe, humanity, and our faith. The truth of scripture can help erode many false beliefs of superiority—for example, the notion that all Africans were heathens who knew nothing about God until European and American missionaries arrived!

The Bible is a multiethnic and multicultural book that has a historical framework consistent with archeological findings. Anthropologists theorize that all humans can trace their lineage to Africa. The Human Genome Project found that all human beings are genetically 99.9 percent the same! These findings tear down every outdated notion about racial or genetic superiority. Together, God's revelation in scripture and general revelation in scientific discovery reaffirm that we are "one people" just like scripture celebrates.

—ROSHANDA AYANNA WOMACK

TODAY

Reimagine Bible stories with people of color as the main characters.

ONE MISSION

"The Spirit of the Lord is on me, because he has anointed me to proclaim good news to the poor." (Luke 4:18)

In 2020, I found myself in a unique position to witness how several churches responded to the societal inequities and racial disparities the pandemic revealed. Being a woman of color in a predominantly white denomination, I was praying for a *kairos* moment: where the Church at large would do the right thing. I waited for the Church to be a prophetic voice, giving righteous and godly direction. Unfortunately, that moment never came. I heard very few pastors speak from the pulpit on the seriousness of COVID-19, its effect on minority communities, or the importance of following safety precautions. Some pastors were reluctant to share sermons on Christlike responses to police brutality, or the wild conspiracy theories that took hold of their congregations, for fear of backlash. Few were bold enough to preach sermons directly aimed at shattering the illusions many of my White Christian brothers and sisters held dear.

To accomplish the prophetic tasks of the Church, we must strive to be on a mission with Christ. In Luke 4:18–19, Jesus shared his mission statement. The first item on his agenda was "to preach good news to the poor." I imagine good news to the poor looks like a world operating without fear or scarcity. A place where everyone has what they need to thrive: food, clean water, housing, clothing, safety, healthcare, education and living wages. Jesus' mission was social, political, and spiritual. Our sermons should be too.

—ROSHANDA AYANNA WOMACK

--- TODAY ---

Be sure to align your messages with Christ's mission.

ONE VOICE

They will turn their ears away from the truth and turn aside to myths. (2 Tim. 4:4)

The renowned Old Testament scholar Walter Brueggemann has a quote that causes me great consternation. I am drawn back to it again and again to wrestle with how to practically apply his words to my life and ministry. He said, "The prophetic tasks of the church are to tell the truth in a society that lives in illusion, grieve in a society that practices denial, and express hope in a society that lives in despair."

I've focused much of our time this week on the ability to know the truth about ourselves and the truth revealed in scripture. We live in a world where there is no longer any sense of absolute truth. Usually, the only "truths" we want to hear are the ones that reinforce what we already believe. People come to church looking for teaching that makes them feel comfortable and right.

As a pastor, it can be a daunting task to preach a message that disturbs people's sense of security and questions their perspectives on reality. But that is exactly what we are called to do. The prophetic voice is necessary to speak directly to the racialized power imbalances within Church and nation. Speaking the truth opens the door for courageous conversations, critical thinking, and deeper Bible study for your congregants. With one voice, we preach truth to open the eyes of saints and soften the hearts of sinners.

—ROSHANDA AYANNA WOMACK

TODAY

Ask what keeps you from using your prophetic voice to confront oppression.

ONE LOVE

Greater love has no one than this: to lay down one's life for one's friends. (John 15:13)

When George Floyd was murdered by a police officer in 2020, a pastor friend called my husband and asked, "What can I do?" My husband replied, "Show up." With this simple statement, he emphasized the importance of being present and acknowledging other people's experiences and pain.

People all over the world stopped what they were doing to show up in solidarity against police brutality. They showed up to march and protest, to write letters, make phone calls, and send emails to their government officials. They "showed up" to demand justice for George Floyd, Breonna Taylor, and countless others who were senselessly murdered. Their presence was an expression of great love. That's what real love looks like: action.

John made it clear that love requires sacrifice, sometimes even to the point of giving one's own life. But do we truly get it? As Christ followers, we are called to be a people known by our love. When we lack sacrificial love, it has a devastating effect on our ability to lament with others. Injustice should always break our hearts.

If we hope to reach diverse communities, we have to be concerned about their real-life experiences. It's hard to get to a place of lament when we become self-centered. It's easy, however, to grieve with and show empathy for others when we value their lives! The Bible teaches us to grieve with those who grieve and to bear each other's burdens. This is how we demonstrate sincere love.

—ROSHANDA AYANNA WOMACK

TODAY

Lament with others by supporting those affected
by unjust policies and practices.

ONE HEART

All this is from God, who reconciled us to himself through Christ
and gave us the ministry of reconciliation. (2 Cor. 5:18)

My husband Todd and I had an African wedding. We wore traditional African attire; we had African drummers and dancers. We included many customs, but my favorite part of the ceremony was the ring exchange. We selected matching gold bands with Ghanaian *Adinkra* symbols. My favorite symbol on our rings is called *Osram Ne Nsoromma*, the moon and the star. It represents faithfulness, love, kindness, and devotion. The love that my husband and I professed for one another is the same type of enduring love we should have as we serve our communities. Unconditional *agape* love is rare. On our own we could never accomplish it, but I thank God, we are not on our own. We have the Holy Spirit who gives us the power to love unselfishly, with "no strings attached."

God's love changes people, communities, and the world. It also changes us, giving us newly found boldness to act and courage to speak, deepening our compassion and our desire for truth. I'm grateful God has chosen us to be ministers of love and reconciliation.

PRAYER

Heavenly Father, give us hearts that break over injustice
wherever we find it. Help us to preach the truth, to practice love
and lament, and to share the hope we have in you. Amen.

REV. ROSHANDA "SHANI" WOMACK, MA, LLPC
is an ordained elder in the Church of the Nazarene. She co-pastors
The Underground, along with her husband, Todd Womack. Together they
have three sons, Ngozi, Osei, and Ande. She is a clinical counselor in
Flint, Michigan, USA. Roshanda is also an artivist who uses
singing and storytelling to promote social justice.

OUTSIDE THE BOX

Therefore go and make disciples of all nations, baptizing them in the name of
the Father and of the Son and of the Holy Spirit, and teaching them to
obey everything I have commanded you. (Matt. 28:19–20)

When I was in college, I knew without a doubt God called me into ministry. However, I struggled as I watched my classmates declare with confidence that they were going to be lead pastors or children's pastors or any other kind of specific ministry. I wrestled with God because I knew I was called to serve the Church, but I didn't have the same convictions as my classmates. I wanted to fit "in a box," but I didn't fit.

What I knew was that my life had been transformed by the grace of God that I experienced in the Church. I knew God had created me to help others experience the grace and new life that I had experienced. On my search for clarity in my calling, I was privileged to spend two summers serving with missionaries in Eastern Europe. I saw the Church in action in incredible ways. The Church was meeting the needs of people in their communities, showing people the love of Jesus, and doing it in ways that didn't fit in any "box" I had seen before.

It was there that I finally began to have clarity in my calling. God showed me that I was made to do the creative work of missions, but that the Church in North America was desperate for new and creative ways to show people the love of Christ. I didn't have the language of church planting then, but the Great Commission came alive in a new way to me.

Church planting is the fulfillment of the Great Commission right in our own neighborhoods and communities in ways that don't always fit in a neat and tidy "box." Not everyone is called to be the one who plants a church, but we are all called to step "outside the box" every now and then to show people God's love in new ways.

—DANA FRANCHETTI

TODAY

Ask God to call you "outside the box" to share his love with others.

CREATIVITY ON MISSION

For we are God's handiwork, created in Christ Jesus to do good works,
which God prepared in advance for us to do. (Eph. 2:10)

One time, I took my friend's teenage daughter to see a musical. She and I share a love of theater, and we had been looking forward to the premiere of this musical for almost two years. As we got settled in our seats, I leaned over to her and said, "Hey, I don't know what it is about musicals, but I will cry." And sure enough, the lights went dark, the beat started for the opening number, and tears were streaming down my face. We laughed because it was absurd.

Have you ever had an experience like this? Maybe it wasn't crying at a musical; maybe it was being overcome with joy at witnessing someone solve a problem or learn a new skill. Maybe it's the rush of adrenaline during a brainstorming session or a sense of peace in an art gallery.

I am convinced that we have such reactions to creativity because we are made in the image of a creative God. The truth is that God has created you for a purpose. You have been given exactly what you need to live out your God-given calling to partner with him in creative ways to show people the grace and truth of Jesus.

—DANA FRANCHETTI

 TODAY

Lean into every one of your creative, God-given gifts.

PASS iT ON

How, then, can they call on the one they have not believed in? And how can they believe in the one of whom they have not heard? And how can they hear without someone preaching to them? And how can anyone preach unless they are sent? As it is written: "How beautiful are the feet of those who bring good news!" (Rom. 10:14–15)

I was part of a group recently where a few people were grieving pastoral transitions happening at their church. They were concerned about how important aspects of ministry would happen without those pastors. It was an incredible moment of grace to witness when the conversation evolved from lament to excitement as they realized the pastors had been preparing and equipping them for the changes ahead. They had already been living out these ministries in their lives.

The group began expressing a sense of calling and responsibility for their church, telling stories of how they were starting small groups with their neighbors who wouldn't step foot in a church building, or serving the parents of their kids' friends, and so much more. Not only that, the goodness was spreading! The groups were multiplying because neighbors were inviting neighbors. They were serving across their community and, best of all, the kids were picking up on it and doing the same.

This is the kingdom of God at work. This is not only discipleship; it is also the start of church multiplication. This group of faithful women just needed to see that they had been equipped, that they are sent to do the good work of sharing the gospel where God has placed them. Often, church planting and multiplication begins when leaders look other leaders in the eyes and help them see what God has gifted them with and called them to do.

—DANA FRANCHETTI

TODAY

Identify a leader; tell them what you see.

STARTING POINT

Also, seek the peace and prosperity of the city to which I have carried you into exile. Pray to the LORD for it, because if it prospers, you too will prosper. (Jer. 29:7)

It was a truly desperate prayer: "God, send me anywhere but rural Texas." So, naturally, I spent four wonderful years in ministry in rural Texas. Have you ever been sent into a situation that felt a bit like exile? Maybe it was a literal move, or maybe it was a season of life? Often, it's easy to see exile as something simply to suffer through and get over with. But what if, in exile, you lean into your faith and trust in God? What might happen if you pay attention to where God has you in all seasons and join in God's good work?

The truth is, whether you are exactly where you want to be or you are stuck in exile wandering around, you are called to work for good in the places around you for the people around you.

I didn't want to move to rural Texas, and I am going to be honest, it was one of the hardest things I have ever done. But when I finally trusted God enough to do the work that he called me to in that place, he showed me the grace that it is to serve and be served, and the kingdom of God came alive in new ways.

—DANA FRANCHETTI

TODAY

Pray for God's eyes to see how to practice peace in your city.

LET THE WORK BEGIN

Do not despise these small beginnings, for the LORD
rejoices to see the work begin. (Zech. 4:10 NLT)

She had no idea that such a simple act of kindness would have such long-lasting implications. She had no idea because hospitality was deeply rooted in her faith; it was as natural to her as breathing. So when she became aware that her new neighbor was working through very intense postpartum depression, with no friends or family nearby, of course she was going to check in on her a few times a week. Obviously, she was going to invite her and the baby over once a week to talk and give the new mother a little break.

She had no idea that those simple acts of kindness would give her neighbor the strength to go to the doctor and get well, and they would lead to the start of a Bible study. Those simple acts of kindness planted seeds of God's grace in the life of that young mother and transformed the family's trajectory for generations.

When it comes to ministry, we love to tell stories of hundreds of people coming to faith in one day, or stories of big, obvious miracles; those are wonderful things. However, the work of the Church is way more about small beginnings. Small beginnings—the beginnings of new relationships, moments of service to others, and taking those small but sometimes scary leaps of faith—are the moments and choices that God uses to build the Church.

—DANA FRANCHETTI

TODAY

Start something small and celebrate with God.

GOD WHO MAKES THINGS GROW

I planted the seed, Apollos watered it, but God has been making it grow.
So neither the one who plants nor the one who waters is anything,
but only God, who makes things grow. (1 Cor. 3:6–7)

Several years ago, I was in a group that had the opportunity to learn from some missionaries who were doing innovative and faithful work. Someone asked them how they stayed healthy and energized after so many years of ministry. Their response was, "We learned a long time ago that God has been at work in these places long before we ever got here, and God will continue to be at work long after we are gone. The fruits of faithfulness that we get to participate in are a huge blessing, but we also know that there will be fruits we may never see."

Paul was teaching a lesson that takes many of us a lifetime to learn. One truth that will keep you grounded is that God is doing the work that God promises to do. In your calling, you are invited to join with God in work that God is doing in your community, but the pressure is off! You aren't called to force fruit to grow. You are called to plant seeds on ground that God has already been tilling and then trust the Spirit to keep working once you are gone. You are called to invest in whomever may be like an Apollos in your life and live openhanded enough to celebrate together, however God works it out.

—DANA FRANCHETTI

TODAY

Pray for eyes to see where God is tilling the ground, and go plant seeds.

THE GREATEST CELEBRATION

After this I looked, and there before me was a great multitude that no one could count, from every nation, tribe, people and language, standing before the throne and before the Lamb. They were wearing white robes and were holding palm branches in their hands. (Rev. 7:9)

One of my favorite realizations about the Church all over the world is that even though we may be separated by distance, culture, experiences, and language, we are unified as members of the Body of Christ, and in that unity, we share certain words, like "hallelujah" or "amen."

God's vision for the Body of Christ is that every person from every background would be unified in celebrating the grace and goodness of God. In the book of Revelation we are given this image for a cosmic celebration that transcends all dividing walls, as the Apostle Paul puts it. It is a beautiful image of what is to come.

But my favorite part about this passage is that it isn't just a picture of what is to come, it is a picture of what could be now! Sisters, you and I are invited to tear down the walls that divide our world and reach across dividing lines to help all people experience the fullness of life that is depicted in Revelation. When we plant churches, or multiply small groups, or reach out to people who are disconnected from the church and community, we are pulling back the curtain and sharing glimpses of God's inviting kingdom.

PRAYER

God, I am so grateful for this invitation to join in the good work you are doing on earth as it is in heaven. Give me eyes to see where you are tilling the ground in the world. Give me the courage to join in this work, and the faith to know that you are at work in all things. Amen.

REV. DANA FRANCHETTI

recently moved to plant a church in Groveland, Florida, USA. Previously, she was lead pastor in Canton, Ohio; children and youth ministry director at Cactus Nazarene Ministry Center working with refugees and immigrants; and executive pastor of mission at New Life Church of the Nazarene in Medford, Oregon.

GOD'S EAGER MERCY

Can a mother forget the baby at her breast and have no compassion on the child she has borne? Though she may forget, I will not forget you! (Isa. 49:15)

A friend at work regaled me with stories of her sister over lunch one day, including funny things they said and did in childhood, complete with the reactions of their parents. Then my friend got quiet and mentioned that she missed her sister. I wondered if this beloved person was still around or if she had she moved away. But my friend informed me that her sister had not spoken a word to her in ten years. Worst of all, they lived right down the street from each other. Whatever caused the breach, this family had lost years of laughing together and the joy of relationship.

If you and I see how tragic this situation is, how much more does God see it, who created us to love and be loved? And how much less likely is God to act the same way? God does not live "right down the street" and refuse to talk to us because of something we've said or done.

The message throughout scripture is that, far from being easily offended or bitter or distant, God reaches out to those who have caused a breach. God does not write you off, does not ignore your voice, does not abandon you when you're difficult—even when you have done all those things to God. As Isaiah wrote, God remembers us more intensely than a nursing mother who has been away from her hungry baby too long.

—KRISTINA LaCELLE-PETERSON

TODAY

Receive the eager mercy of God who remembers you and forgets your failures.

THE BROKENHEARTED CRY OF A PARENT

"O my son Absalom! My son, my son Absalom! If only I had died
instead of you—O Absalom, my son, my son!" (2 Sam. 18:33)

A number of years ago, a young man with a gun went on a rampage in an Amish schoolhouse. As the world looked on in anguish and amazement, the Amish community publicly announced their forgiveness of this man. Ultimately, they even gathered funds together to pay for the shooter's funeral, so that his wife didn't have to bear that burden on top of everything else. Many people were shocked by this response, given our cultural habit of thinking that a criminal should be punished to the full extent of the law. We have been conditioned to think of retribution before mercy, and the drive to punish rather than to forgive.

Sadly, sometimes we project onto God our zeal for punishment. According to a recent Pew Research survey, when most Americans hear the word *God* they think of anger. In popular imagination, God is pictured as a terrifying judge meting out justice. But the Bible reveals God more like the brokenhearted David longing for his wayward son than as a cold, distant judge.

The pathos of David's words should ring in our ears, because it points to the great lengths to which God is willing to go to express love for us. Jesus comes all the way to join in our humanity, and even died for us, to demonstrate God's extravagant mercy and love for us.

—KRISTINA LaCELLE-PETERSON

TODAY

Picture the brokenhearted God next time you expect judgment.

JESUS REJECTS A WOMAN'S UNWORTHINESS

The Samaritan woman said to him, "You are a Jew and I am
a Samaritan woman. How can you ask me for a drink?" (John 4:9)

A young woman had only been living in the United States for a couple of years when she began attending a Christian college. In the course of her music lessons, her older male professor became inappropriately affectionate with her. For months, she suppressed her confusion and frustration, almost assuming that this was simply what women had to put up with. Who was she to accuse this accomplished musician of wrongdoing? Finally, in an emotional conversation with her roommate, it all came out. Her friend listened, she believed, and she encouraged the distraught music student to lodge a formal complaint. By the end of the semester, the college had let that professor go.

It was justice; his wrongdoing was addressed and just treatment and respect were restored to her.

But in this broken world, justice can feel like mercy or even a miracle. So it was for the woman Jesus conversed with at the well. We don't know her backstory, but we do know that she was so theologically astute that, as one scholar observed, if she had been a man, we would assume she herself was a rabbi. Jesus recognized this and engaged her in a theological conversation without patronizing her. He rejected the unworthiness she may have felt as a Samaritan, as a woman, and as a person with a complicated marital history, and he treated her with respect. This was justice but it was also a surprise!

—KRISTINA LaCELLE-PETERSON

TODAY

Be assured, Jesus rejects cultural assumptions about
your unworthiness as a woman.

SEEING PEOPLE

"Do you see this woman?" (Luke 7:44)

Several years ago, a young guy wearing jeans, a T-shirt, and a baseball cap stood near an escalator in a DC Metro station playing his violin. In the forty-three minutes he performed, about a thousand people walked by; only seven stopped to listen. Collectively, they donated about thirty-two dollars. Making thirty-two dollars an hour may not sound bad, but this musician was actually the world-famous violinist Joshua Bell. The previous week, he played a sold-out concert in Boston's Symphony Hall, where tickets for "pretty good" seats sold for a hundred dollars each. Chances are that most busy commuters thought he was just another guy busking for change in the subway, maybe a music school student who couldn't get a job. They didn't truly hear him or see him.

We all use shortcuts to evaluate people; we're busy, so we put people in categories, sometimes failing to see individuals. But Jesus did this woman the justice of really seeing her. He did not reduce her to her sexuality. He did not allow sin to define her. This is such good news—that God sees us for who we are, in all our delightful complexity: the longings, the loves, the successes, the disappointments.

Let's welcome the people around us in the same way, not through stereotypes brought to mind by clothes or tattoos, age or youth, race or accent, but because we stand before the One who truly sees us all.

—KRISTINA LaCELLE-PETERSON

TODAY

As you are seen by Jesus, carefully see those around you.

LEARNING GREAT LOVE

"Therefore, I tell you, her many sins have been forgiven—as her great love
has shown. But whoever has been forgiven little loves little." (Luke 7:47)

Some friends decided to walk the Appalachian Trail. In order to train for it, they began with local hikes carrying partially filled backpacks, increasing the weight each time. On one occasion, the hike included a great deal of climbing. When they reached the summit, the young woman with the largest pack sank down in relief; the one who appeared to be carrying the most was the most delighted when she could lay it down. But as it turned out, one of the other women had a much heavier load, though carried in a smaller pack.

In Luke's story, the problem isn't that the woman was a worse sinner but that her failings were publicly known. She carried a bigger backpack, as it were, relieved to lay it down. In our day, sexual sins still draw extra attention, as if sexuality is the only arena of human life that God is concerned with. Like the host in Luke 7, we may overlook the whole range of internal failings that so often plague religious folks, things like envy, impatience, or an inordinate need to be right. In short, we may fail to love others (or ourselves) as we should.

Whether you're carrying the burden of a sin you never thought you could commit or the chronic bad attitudes stemming from imperfect love, you can lay down whatever load you carry. Then comes the great love.

—KRISTINA LaCELLE-PETERSON

TODAY

Let this woman be an example: confident of Jesus' mercy, she repented.

FORGIVENESS LEADS TO SERVICE

"Simon son of John, do you love me?" . . . Jesus said, "Feed my sheep." (John 21:17)

In the early 1800s, a young African American woman named Jarena Lee felt called to preach. Like other Methodist leaders at that time, Richard Allen, the founder of the AME church, refused to endorse the preaching of a woman. In her autobiography, Jarena Lee exclaimed, "Is Jesus only half a Savior?" by which she showed how deeply connected forgiveness and calling are.

Jesus saves us *from* something—sin—but also saves us *for* something—employment in God's vineyard. After agonizing years of staying silent, Jarena Lee finally spoke one Sunday morning. The scheduled preacher announced that he "lost the Spirit," at which point Jarena Lee jumped up and gave a powerful sermon on Jonah, applying it to her life. To his credit, Richard Allen admitted that he had been wrong about women being called to preach.

Is Jesus only half a Savior? Is God only concerned with forgiveness of sin? Certainly not, since the restoration of all things is the ultimate goal. Scripture declares that even punishment can serve that end. Exile, after all, leads to return, and forgiveness naturally points beyond the mending of relationship to a renewed participation in God's work. Consider the case of Peter. After forgiving him, Jesus moved on to the next step: reiteration of the call. Jesus' message to Peter can be summarized, "If you have repented, if you love me, then don't be bogged down with the past, but do the work I put in your hands."

—KRISTINA LaCELLE-PETERSON

TODAY

Hear Jesus, the whole Savior, invite your love and service again today.

WASHED UP, READY

Wash and make yourselves clean. . . . Learn to do right; seek justice.
Defend the oppressed. (Isa. 1:16–17)

The sixteenth-century mystic Teresa of Avila compared the soul to an interior castle into which we gradually allow Jesus to come. As we mature spiritually, we open more rooms to his presence. For many of us, when we invite someone into our domestic space, we have a compelling impulse to clean; and the more important the visitor, the deeper the cleaning.

"Wash yourselves," Isaiah says. Clean out all the things that stand in the way of love. To stay with Teresa's metaphor, if someone were not only to visit but to come and live with you, you might try to guess a color scheme or furniture arrangement that would make the person feel most at home. You might make your space reflect the preferences of your guest.

What does our Guest prefer?

Hearts so full of love there isn't room for anything else. Love that expresses itself in kindness and in active interest in the joys and sorrows of others. Love that promotes the just treatment of all people and works to restore all those oppressed by unjust people and systems. Let's wash up, join our Guest, and begin to learn the craft of justice.

 PRAYER

Gracious and holy God, thank you for reaching out to this world in love. Draw me in again; wash me clean, ready to seek justice and show mercy. Form your character in me as I learn to imitate more fully the loving life of Jesus. Amen.

DR. KRISTINA LaCELLE-PETERSON

is professor of religion at Houghton College. She lives in Rochester, New York, USA. She is on the periodic preaching rotation at Community of the Savior, a Free Methodist congregation. She lives within a couple of miles of where Susan B. Anthony lived and worked toward the full equality of women before the law. Dr. LaCelle-Peterson is the author of *Liberating Tradition: Women's Identity and Vocation in Christian Perspective*.

CALLED TO LEAD

CALLED OUT

As a prisoner for the Lord, then, I urge you to live a life
worthy of the calling you have received. (Eph. 4:1)

Summer evenings in my childhood were for endlessly playing "Eenie Aye Over" (or "Ante Over"). The game involved neighborhood kids throwing a tennis ball over a house to an opposing team and then chasing each other around the house. Did you ever play? As darkness fell, we tried hard not to hear Allene Jackson's distinct whistle that called her kids home.

Sadly, most women I know who have been summoned by God to fulfill a pastoral calling have quietly or loudly resisted the call at first. Apparently, many still fight the same internal battle I fought fifty years ago! What could God's call really mean?

I had never met a female pastor. The only women I had seen in the pulpit were missionaries. A few biblical texts seemed to paint a picture of God frowning on women's leadership. The bold, liberating stance of my denomination's founder had been completely lost, so a woman's call was often questioned, doubted, and analyzed to death. I got stuck in that cycle for twelve years.

Listen up, sister! If God has called you (and God has a unique, distinctive "whistle"—you'll hear it), rise up and run toward it! Whatever game you're in the middle of, God's invitation is to a life that is higher, better, and infinitely more rewarding than that game. Receive God's call gladly and live a life worthy of the incomparable privilege of serving God.

—LINDA ADAMS

TODAY

Verify and clarify God's call, and reaffirm your "Yes!"

WHEN IN DOUBT, GO LOW

Be completely humble and gentle; be patient, bearing with one another in love. (Eph. 4:2)

"But he's just a regular guy!" New Hope Church was hosting a distinguished visitor, Bishop Richard Snyder. He showed up dressed in a suit and tie, not a "bright red robe and a pointy hat," as some of our newer people had expected.

Even more surprising to some was his demeanor—the twinkle in his eye and shy smile on his face. When he preached, he couldn't hold back tears. His message had a prophetic edge, but he was a weeping prophet, not a judgmental, bombastic, or arrogant prophet. People were drawn to him.

To live a life worthy of the calling we have received, the Apostle Paul points us downward. The word "humility" is derived from *humus,* meaning earth or ground. God created humans (there's that root word again!) from the earth or, in the case of Eve, from the side of the human who had come from the earth. Accepting our common humanity, flaws and all, prevents us from ever posturing over others as leaders.

Leading relationally from a posture of complete humility, gentleness, and patient love is to recognize our lowliness, just like Mary showed awareness of hers. At the moment of her greatest exaltation, she proclaimed, "He has been mindful of the humble state of his servant" (Luke 1:48).

Think about the leaders you most admire. For me, humility, gentleness, and patient love are the crowning qualities of Jesus-following leaders.

—LINDA ADAMS

TODAY

Be humble; trust God to do the exalting.

20/20 VISION

Make every effort to keep the unity of the Spirit through the bond of peace. (Eph. 4:3)

Lots of us who speak English as a first language prepared for 2020 with wordplay on having "20/20 vision"—optometrist language for perfect eyesight. We were ready with our eyesight themes: clarity, unity, focus. As a Christian leader, were you as optimistic as I was?

But what 2020 brought—and 2021 continued—was exactly the opposite: "division." Not one coherent ability to perceive biblically and well, but a multiplicity of competing visions, claims, and frantic imperatives to steer congregations this way and that in response to world events. The division in our churches has been damaging and exhausting.

As the Apostle Paul prepares to celebrate the diversity of the body, he sets it up with a call to unity. The unity of the Spirit is something to be preserved, kept through our very best efforts. In fact, we should spare no effort to preserve it—to do absolutely everything in our power.

The Holy Spirit has been given to create supernatural oneness among believers, deriving from the oneness of the Godhead. We can sustain that oneness as we live in peace with one another through Christ Jesus, who is himself our peace (Eph. 2:14).

Can we find a way to bridge twenty-first century divides? The answer comes from an author who was likely in chains, in bonds for the Gospel. The Apostle Paul said that peace can be what bonds us together; in fact, we can be bonded together by the peace of Jesus and experience unity. Let's pray for this.

—LINDA ADAMS

TODAY

Work for oneness with other believers through Christ, who is our peace.

DO YOU HAVE HOPE?

There is one body and one Spirit, just as you were called
to one hope when you were called. (Eph. 4:4)

A few years ago, our family visited Dachau, the infamous Nazi concentration camp. Its sheer size and efficient design, gas chambers, and crematoria still silently testify to its horrors.

Corrie ten Boom, a survivor of Ravensbrück camp, described an unforgettable scene of hope. In the midst of despair, she wrote in *The Hiding Place* about huddling with a few women to read the Bible, "like waifs clustered around a blazing fire . . . holding out our hearts to its warmth and light. The blacker the night around us grew, the brighter and truer and more beautiful burned the Word of God. . . . Sometimes I would slip the Bible from its little sack with hands that shook, so mysterious had it become to me," she wrote. It was as if "it was new; it had just been written. I marveled sometimes that the ink was dry."

What warmth and light emanated from God's Word to overcome the chill of cruelty and death? In such a grim place, a hopeless, dead-end scenario, God's Spirit and Word infused these women with supernatural hope.

As one body, through one Spirit, we access the one and only hope in the universe. Our hope is in the Lord, in the Gospel, in the promise that God will bring history to his own end and is even now preparing a place for his beloved. No matter how dark things get, we are called to be agents of hope.

—LINDA ADAMS

TODAY

Hope in God and God alone.

BUILDING THE BODY OF CHRIST

So Christ himself gave the apostles, the prophets, the evangelists,
the pastors and teachers, to equip his people for works of service,
so that the body of Christ may be built up. (Eph. 4:11–12)

One of the most exciting realities in scripture is that Christ himself is the one who gives spiritual gifts, and this gracious distribution is not based on gender. Christ gives gifted *people* to the Church, to build it up through equipping. These leaders are God's gift to the Church. Their gifts are not for their own sake but for the good of others and ultimately the glory of God.

Once we grasp that God's gifts are not assigned according to gender, we discover that the Spirit of God has filled and anointed women throughout salvation history to speak and act on his behalf. Some of them are such hidden gems!

For instance, Huldah was a prophet, a contemporary of Jeremiah, but when young King Josiah needed to consult the Lord, his advisors chose her (see 2 Kings 22:14–20). Paul's greetings in Romans 16 include more female colleagues than any list in antiquity: Phoebe, the deacon and benefactor; Priscilla, the teacher who risked her life for Paul; Mary, who worked hard for the church; Junia, the apostle; Tryphena and Tryphosa and Persis, who "worked hard in the Lord"; Rufus' mother, who was "a mother" to Paul, Julia, and Nereus' sister. (Who knew about *her*?)

Praise God for the divine wisdom that freely gives spiritual gifts of leadership in the kingdom enterprise!

—LINDA ADAMS

TODAY

Develop and use your gifts to equip God's people to do good.

NO LiES HERE

Then we will no longer be infants, tossed back and forth by the waves,
and blown here and there by every wind of teaching and by the cunning
and craftiness of people in their deceitful scheming. (Eph. 4:14)

Are you a "glass half-full" optimistic kind of person? I am; I've always wanted to believe the best of people.

Unfortunately, people like us have to be awakened to the truth that some people are cunning and crafty, as this text describes. Some collude together in "deceitful scheming." Their aim is deliberate deception of the naïve and the immature. Here, Paul calls immature believers "infants"; they lack the maturity and judgment to discern error. When winds of false teaching blow, they are helpless.

The past few years have seen the rise of social media posts and television programming promoting false prophecies and false teaching. I'm sure you know people who believe these lies and are being led astray. I do.

God's design for the Church is that we mature together as local expressions of the Body of Christ. That we outgrow our baby, childhood, and adolescent stages, until we "all reach unity in the faith and in the knowledge of the Son of God and become mature, attaining to the whole measure of the fullness of Christ" (Eph. 4:13).

Whether you're a pastor or a member of a local expression of the Body of Christ, press in toward unity and knowing Jesus better together. God intends to use you to equip others to grow up and withstand the winds and waves of deception. I pray you'll find a few others to sail together on these high seas.

—LiNDA ADAMS

TODAY

Find a few others who will help you know Jesus better.

GROWING INTO THE PERFECT BODY

Instead, speaking the truth in love, we will grow to become in every respect the mature body of him who is the head, that is, Christ. (Eph. 4:15)

Almost everyone I know has a complaint about their body. It seems we've all compared ourselves with some supposed ideal and decided we're too tall or too short, too stocky or too thin, too curly-haired or too straight-haired, that even our nose isn't right! There's not only a giant plastic surgery industry but even television shows so we can watch the sculpting "perfection" happen, or watch one surgeon fix another's botched operation!

Rather than wallow in complaints about our physical bodies, how about this better obsession? Be amazed you've been given the privilege of growing into the spiritual body of the Perfect One. Our aim as serious Christ followers is to pursue our relationship with God to maturity. That Greek word for *mature* also means "complete" and "perfect." We Wesleyans celebrate this call to come "further up and further in."

It isn't a solitary venture; it's lived in the context of community. It's about relationships of truth and love—specifically, of telling the truth in a loving way. As we tell ourselves and one another the honest truth about God and ourselves, we grow. We grow together, in unity, in love. This is God's brilliant design, and we get to participate.

PRAYER

Gracious God, I'm awed to share in your Body and your work in the world.
Help us all grow into maturity until we reach the unity you
want for us. In Jesus' name. Amen.

BISHOP LINDA ADAMS
has served as the Bishop of the Free Methodist Church (FMC) since 2019. Over her thirty years of ministry, she has also served in local churches as well as the director of International Child Care Ministries, the child sponsorship ministry of the FMC. Linda likes to swim, cook, play the piano, and travel. She has two children.

A CALL TO LEAD

David said to Saul, "Let no one lose heart on account of this Philistine;
your servant will go and fight him." (1 Sam. 17:32)

There are catalytic moments in our lives when a situation stirs something in our hearts that causes us to rise up and lead. Often, however, we pause to take a mental tally of our gifts, abilities, and strengths, and begin to conclude that we're lacking. Our courage falters; we take a step back with confusion about our calling and identity as God's anointed.

As the entire Israelite army cowered in terror, David did not hesitate to brave the challenge of the Philistine giant. He determined that the threat of Goliath, the corresponding fear of the soldiers, and his own combat skills were all inconsequential to the matters at hand. What was of utmost importance to David was that this was God's battle, not his. Goliath was mighty, but God was all-powerful.

As women in leadership, many of us have struggled with overcoming our own giants. The world reflects our inadequacies back to us through messages of disapproval. How much evidence do we need to believe for ourselves that God delights in using the underestimated to bring down the powerful? It is God's favored tactical approach. We see this all over scripture. God wills to use you in the same way. It is to God's great pleasure that you are his way of fulfilling his good purpose. Let's marvel in that!

—CHRISTINE YOUN HUNG

TODAY

Find cheer in trusting God's call on your life.

THE INEVITABILITY OF DISAPPROVAL

When Eliab, David's oldest brother, heard him speaking with the men, he burned with anger at him and asked, "Why have you come down here?" (1 Sam 17:28)

There is a cultural tendency for people to set expectations and boundaries on those in leadership. It is a constant push and pull as voices clamor for us to lead the way but push back if we direct them to uncomfortable places that challenge the status quo. The hazards of leadership, especially as we navigate these days, come with the inevitability of disapproval. In fact, Ronald Heifetz, a leading voice in leadership theory, says that an essential role of a leader is to help people tolerate the discomfort that comes with the disruption of development and change.

David's own brother, Eliab, criticized David for operating beyond his responsibilities of watching sheep. Eliab's anger clouded any gratitude or recognition that their father had sent David to bring food for his brothers. And worse, Eliab's anger obscured his understanding of God's ability to use David to lead the army to victory.

Discipling the people of God into the countercultural way of God's kingdom has always come with an ensuing response of grumbling protest. But, as God is in the business of making all things new, there is an implicit understanding that God calls leaders to guide their people into divine possibilities, dreaming dreams that are beyond the world's rationale.

Managing the disapproval of others means taking the time to prayerfully discern God's leading in each circumstance. It means to walk confidently in the path of God's will, even in the face of opposition.

—CHRISTINE YOUN HUNG

TODAY

Stand firm in God's direction with boldness and grace.

STRENGTH TRAINING THROUGH ADVERSITY

"The LORD who rescued me from the paw of the lion and the paw of the bear will rescue me from the hand of this Philistine." (1 Sam. 17:37)

We have heard it said that God is more concerned about changing our hearts than changing our circumstances. Arguably, our hearts would never be changed without the challenges that come with the very circumstances we long to avoid.

In the same way that strength training from one workout makes us stronger for the next workout, overcoming difficult obstacles in present circumstances will help us face future obstacles tomorrow. However, it is not simply about exercising our spiritual muscles.

There is something about our personal valley of dry bones: we learn to die to ourselves. We learn to stop striving in our own efforts, for our own earthly preoccupations or goals.

When the challenge of Goliath was presented to him, David ruminated on his own past encounters against formidable opponents while tending his flock. It was by the hand of God that David was able to defeat these mighty predators. For David, it was without doubt that God was the one who rescued him in his time of need. It was without doubt that God would rescue him now, in the threat of this new adversary.

The lessons we learn through past adversity and suffering strengthen us for what we face today. How important it is to look back and reflect on God's faithfulness to refine and prepare you, especially as you lead people to do the same.

—CHRISTINE YOUN HUNG

TODAY

Take heart that God is strengthening you and won't waste adversity.

RESISTING THE WEIGHT OF EXPECTATION

Then Saul dressed David in his own tunic. He put a coat of armor on him. . . .
"I cannot go in these," he said to Saul. (1 Sam. 17:38–39)

In leadership, it is often a struggle to form our identities without being influenced by the world's "cookie cutter" standards of what it looks like to be an effective leader. Instead of developing a voice that is uniquely your own, it's easy to imitate voices amplified by successful platforms or echoing through the hall of past greats.

Imagine David, the youngest of eight sons and not yet a man of war, outfitted with King Saul's tunic and armor, a heavy sword in hand. The king had the best of intentions, to be sure. It was unthinkable to send this young shepherd boy out to be slaughtered without the best armor to protect him. David, however, found the suit ill-fitting and unfamiliar. He must have understood the honor of bearing the king's armor upon his own shoulders, yet he chose to go without. David stepped out into the battlefield having full confidence in his identity as God's child and not the king's chosen.

When we insist on leading under the weight of others' expectations, it is like battling in an ill-fitted suit of armor. When you compare yourself with others, you will lose sight of your own distinctiveness. Only when you embrace your God-given identity are you able to freely lead in the unique and beautiful way God designed you to lead.

—CHRISTINE YOUN HUNG

TODAY

Lean into God's unique design for your identity as a leader.

IN THE NAME OF THE LORD ALMIGHTY

David said to the Philistine, "You come against me with sword and spear and javelin, but I come against you in the name of the LORD Almighty." (1 Sam. 17:45)

As leaders, we are constantly being challenged by life's many obstacles—some internal, some external. Some of us are facing insecurity, self-doubt, mental or physical health problems, broken marriages, or family issues. Some of us are facing systemic injustice, economic scarcity, toxic circumstances, or broken systems. Some of us are facing real, in-person opponents in our ministries or workplaces who aim to dishearten and discourage us. It is easy to be overwhelmed by these challenges, especially when we see ourselves as the underdog. We cannot imagine how we are to defeat these formidable adversaries.

David faced Goliath. The Philistine giant's height and girth terrified the Israelite army. David, however, eyed the seasoned war hero's stature—his impressive armor and weapons—with an unshaken demeanor. Goliath bore not only a sword, but a spear and javelin as well. Only five smooth stones and a sling were held in David's hands as he ran to the battle line. But David knew that his strength was not in five stones. He was coming against the giant in the name of the Lord Almighty.

As you confront your weapon-bearing adversaries, you must determine what you are fighting for. David stood against Goliath because the Philistines were defying God. Are you fighting for the same reason or simply defending your own agenda? When God calls you to fight in his mighty name, he will always be faithful to deliver.

—CHRISTINE YOUN HUNG

TODAY

Be emboldened by the name of the Lord in battle.

BOLD FOR THE GLORY OF GOD

"All those gathered here will know that it is not by sword or spear that the LORD saves; for the battle is the LORD's." (1 Sam. 17:47)

As followers of Jesus, we see that our leadership is defined by God's purposes. God calls us to use our gifts and graces to further the mission of God. The moment we pursue our own ambitions, agendas, and platforms, even if they are worthy ones, we risk diverting away from God's direction for our lives.

David clearly understood that the battle was the Lord's and not his own. He was not there to bring glory to his own name, nor was he there to secure a position for himself in the king's army. David was not even there to defend or protect the people of Israel. David was there to exalt the name of the Lord. He declared that the whole world would know that there was a God in Israel when God delivered Goliath into his hands.

Whether you are leading a church, managing a business, parenting a child, teaching a class, or standing against the injustices of the world, do it for God's glory. Do it because you are partnering in God's work to see all of creation restored and reconciled to God and to each other. As you submit yourself to God's authority and protection, those around you will see God's true authority and power when battles beyond your own capacity are won by his hand.

—CHRISTINE YOUN HUNG

TODAY

Walk boldly in obedience and humility, knowing the battle belongs to God.

BOLDLY LEADING FROM WEAKNESS

But he said to me, "My grace is sufficient for you,
for my power is made perfect in weakness." (2 Cor. 12:9)

The story of David and Goliath teaches us many lessons, the greatest being that God uses weakness for his good purposes.

I used to loathe any signs of weakness in myself. Saying yes to hard things filled me with anxiety; I knew my weaknesses would rise to the surface, causing me great discomfort. I wrestled with God to release me from the work he called me to, but the Lord continued to call, and I continued to respond.

I began to realize, however, the more inadequate I felt at a task, the more desperately I clung to Jesus. The more desperately I clung to Jesus, the more I saw his faithful hand at work in my ministry. This happened so often that I couldn't help but come to embrace my weaknesses.

The measly five stones in your sling, the few loaves and fish in your basket, the oil in your jar, the staff in your hand, are transformed from feeble offerings to powerful battle plans of God's design. How could we not embrace our weaknesses? When you surrender your inadequacy to the Lord, you draw closer to him, revealing to the world God's power made known in weakness!

 PRAYER

Heavenly Father, as we imagine David choosing five smooth stones from the stream, I pray that we would consider what five simple offerings we can surrender to you. May you anoint whatever we have in our hands to do your work in powerful ways and draw us closer to you. Amen.

REV. CHRISTINE YOUN HUNG
is a pastor, writer, speaker, and the director of pastoral development for the Northern California District Church of the Nazarene, USA. She takes deep joy in her husband, Albert, and their four children; she is pursuing a doctorate of ministry in ecclesial mission and leadership.

GOD'S LOVE SHOWN IN OUR UNITY

"I in them and you in me—so that they may be brought to complete unity. Then the world will know that you sent me and have loved them." (John 17:23)

One day, I walked into a church where the whole of its ethnic diversity was created by my presence. I have done this many times in many places as part of my ministry work. Growing up in a multiethnic home, I am used to being around people of various ethnicities, and I am used to shifting my persona for my cultural interactions in order to help others feel a little more comfortable around me.

Occasionally, I've entered a church as a visitor and been questioned about whether I am at the "wrong" church. At other times, I've been completely ignored: not a single person among the two hundred people in the congregation said hello as I entered the sanctuary, joining them for worship. Once in a while, church members have tried to be "helpful" by directing me to a congregation of a different ethnicity down the road.

In the context of this range of experiences visiting churches, we pray the words of Jesus, for the unity of believers across ethnicities and races, so that all people are welcomed into any congregation of Christ followers. We pray that we can just say hello to a person who might appear to be different. Those are only the beginning, small steps toward fully showing God's love. How do we lead others in unity, so that the world sees God's love?

—CARRON ODOKARA

Lead in unity so the world will know Jesus.

THE PASTOR OF EVERYBODY ELSE

"Love your neighbor as yourself." (Luke 10:27)

When I was in college, I attended a congregation in a small building out in the country. The pastor of that congregation was the first female lead pastor I got to know. Pastor Johnson always said that God's focus for her church's ministry was to take in all the people God sent that others might not want. She was the pastor of "everybody else." Her congregation was bursting through the walls with growth. The congregation welcomed a diverse group of people regardless of age, gender, ethnicity, or socioeconomic status.

When it comes to loving our neighbors, think of Jesus' parable in Luke 10:25–37. Jesus described the good Samaritan, who transcended ethnic borders to care for the beaten person on the side of the road. The neighbor to love is the Samaritan, a person that the Jewish people would avoid; but this Samaritan was kind enough to help a stranger. The neighbor to love is the man in need by the side of the road. The neighbors to love were the priest and the Levite, who saw the need and just kept walking.

Most of our congregations already say they welcome and minister to everybody. "Everybody" needs to include those who don't look like us, dress like us, and think like us. Don't forget to love and serve "everybody else" that others might not want.

—CARRON ODOKARA

Be the pastor of everybody—and everybody else.

THE LORD PLANS FOR WHATEVER

Commit to the LORD whatever you do, and he will establish your plans. (Prov. 16:3)

Some of us remember as kids using large paper maps or a paper atlas to plan car trips. Sometimes the maps would wear out, tear, or have partial or out-of-date information. Today, many of us use a GPS; we type in a location, and our route is tracked and directed through each turn until we get to our destination. While technology means less work or inconvenience for travelers, someone still had to create the device and code its programming in order for it to work seamlessly, showing which of all the possible routes will get us to our destination the most quickly.

Proverbs 16:3 reminds us that the Lord's plans are for our work and for all parts of our lives. It's easy to get accustomed to handling things by weighing options and determining what we think the best path to the end goal will be. Some of us who are bivocational get paid and conditioned to handle the planning in our "9 to 5" jobs.

But everything—every part of our lives—needs to be committed to the Lord. When you realize that you are operating with partial information to lead in your ministry, your corporate workplace, your relationships, or your family, committing whatever you do to God becomes even more appealing. This is because you can have the Spirit's presence with you, the direction of the Holy Spirit along your path. Have you committed whatever you do to follow God's lead?

—CARRON ODOKARA

TODAY

Keep moving forward as God illuminates the next step of the path.

1 + 1 + 1 = 1

Just as a body, though one, has many parts, but all its many parts
form one body, so it is with Christ. (1 Cor. 12:12)

Music is a beautiful expression of artistry, exhibiting the gifts and diversity of everyone involved in performance. The conductor of an orchestra stands to guide the instrumentalists through the music. Each musician plays their instrument on cue, according to the arrangement they are playing. The first violins play their part together as a complement to the second violins, the cellos, and all the other instruments. Each instrument's part may be recognizable separately as the melody of the song or in the complementary harmonies. Other instruments may play notes that fill out the overall depth of the orchestra's sound. All of the instruments together build the fullness of the one overall musical experience.

The Body of Christ is similar to the orchestra. In the Body of Christ, we have different gifts. One person has the gift of healing, one person has the gift of helping. Others have gifts of teaching, wisdom, prophecy, and more. All of the gifts work together in harmony to complement one another. Every person brings their gifts to work together in one body.

1 gift + 1 gift + 1 gift = 1 body in Christ

As leaders, we encourage people to recognize their own gifts and utilize them as part of the Body of Christ. How are you encouraging each person to use their gifts in the Body?

—CARRON ODOKARA

TODAY

Encourage people with diverse gifts to work together as one body.

NEXT UP

"Moses my servant is dead. Now then, you and all these people, get ready to cross the Jordan River into the land I am about to give to them." (Josh. 1:2)

In my first leadership position, I stepped into a job replacing a well-liked leader. Comparisons abounded, spoken and unspoken. Apparently, I did everything differently than my predecessor, and most of those things I didn't do as well as he did. Some of the changes may have been due to having a woman in the leadership position; some grumbling was just because I was not my predecessor. It took years for the comparisons to become less frequent, and it took prayers for me to let the comparisons not bother me so much. I was Joshua, and there would never be another Moses. However, there did not need to be another Moses.

This verse from Joshua is encouraging when I am the "Joshua" coming into a new situation and I want people to recognize the departure of my predecessor so that they can be ready to move forward with me. However, I have also experienced the other side of this scenario: when I am like Moses. In that case, I have to recognize that I am done in my current position and need to move on so that someone new can replace me.

Leadership transitions are difficult for the people and the leaders. However, they are necessary for new opportunities and new growth in the paths ahead for everyone. Are you ready for the new possibilities that God has ahead for you?

—CARRON ODOKARA

TODAY

Move from death to new life by leading into God's promised land.

WHOSE HOUSE?

Unless the LORD builds the house, the builders labor in vain. Unless the LORD watches over the city, the guards stand watch in vain. (Ps. 127:1)

Our church was growing and already shifting to two worship services in order to have seating capacity in the sanctuary. Leaders assessed the growing youth ministry and a developing children's ministry. The limitations of the building and property had the church council exploring all types of possibilities. As the leadership continued to discuss the future, an architectural firm was hired to create a master plan; another firm was hired to assist with a capital campaign. The stresses of all of this were overwhelming for the leadership in the continued work for the growing ministries and the daunting prospect of the first phase of building.

I wish this story had the fairytale happy ending with the money to develop the building and the exponential growth of the church and its ministries. However, the architect's master plan remained unfulfilled. We tried to build God's house based on our plans, but that was in vain. It is God's house, and it is God that needs to build it. As we continue to look at the church and its ministries, God's master plan is still being discovered.

As church leaders, we learned that prayer precedes planning, prayer parallels planning, and prayer positions planning for the Lord to build his house. In the first phase of God's new master plan, we are the first house that God wants to build, and the rest comes according to God's design.

—CARRON ODOKARA

TODAY

Pray for God to build his house according to his timing and design.

NEXT-GENERATION DISCIPLE MAKERS

Barnabas took Mark and sailed for Cyprus. (Acts 15:39)

When I was a college student, my pastor asked me to lead the weekly adult Bible study at church. Most of the people there were as old as my mother and grandmother. How could this kid teach the grown-ups anything?

I was terrified but prepared my lesson and stepped up to speak. I don't remember the lesson, but I remember the graciousness of the congregation and the encouragement of the pastor. That small church pastor gave me a chance to minister, like Barnabas gave Mark a chance even after disappointing Paul. God led a Barnabas to disciple me.

Years later, I was the older person, an associate pastor leading a young adult ministry. It was my turn to be a Barnabas to others; I recruited young adult teachers for our weekly studies. As I listened to them teach, I was nervous—and had to bite my tongue a couple times. But the young adults communicated differently, using examples that connected with the others. I was pleased to learn from them.

Encouraging the next generation to be disciples is one step; empowering the next generation of disciple-makers is our next assignment as leaders. Find a Barnabas—and be a Barnabas.

PRAYER

God, thank you for sending a Barnabas to disciple me to become a disciple-making leader. Help me to find the next person to encourage, equip, and empower to lead so that I can be a Barnabas to them. Amen.

REV. DR. CARRON ODOKARA

resides in Michigan, USA. She has been associate pastor at Farmington Hills Church of God while working bivocationally as an IT manager at Ford Motor Company. Carron is president of the Wesleyan Holiness Women Clergy Board of Directors for the 2020–2022 term. She has a bachelor's degree in electrical engineering, a master's degree in computer engineering, and a master of divinity degree and PhD in organizational leadership, examining racial and ethnic diversity and inclusion in Christian denominations.

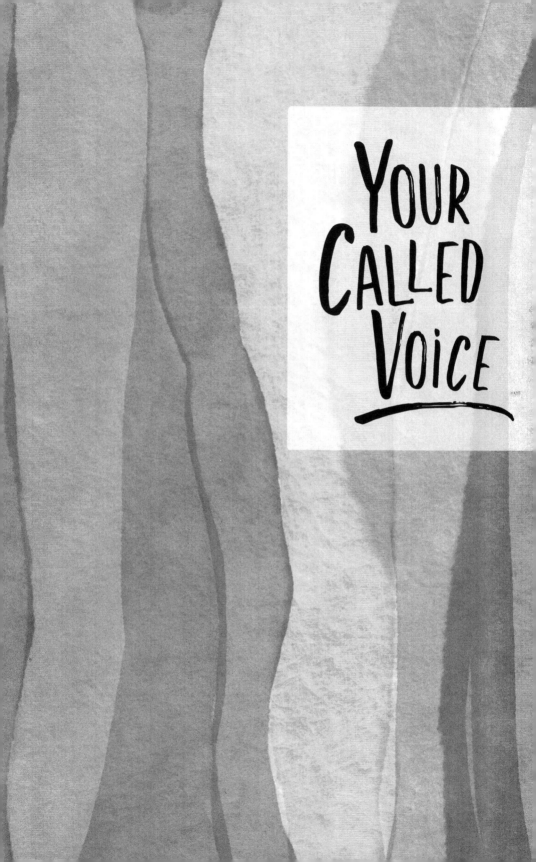

YOUR
CALLED
VOICE